Thunder on the Rocker Road
BIG BRITISH BIKES
OF THE 50s AND 60s

N. Ward.
(no thrashing)

Thunder on the Rocker Road

BIG BRITISH BIKES
OF THE 50s AND 60s

N. Ward (f.s.h)

By Steve Wilson

Photography by Garry Stuart

Herridge & Sons

Published in 2015 by
Herridge & Sons Ltd
Lower Forda, Shebbear,
Beaworthy,
Devon EX21 5SY

Photography by Garry Stuart
Design by Ray Leaning, MUSE Fine Art & Design

ISBN 978-1-906133-60-3
Printed in China

CONTENTS

FOREWORD

Velocette Venom Thruxton was the final development of the Venom, one of the two singles featured in this book.

This book takes a look at the British motorcycles used by riders in the ton-up and Rocker era. Since pre-war days, transport and other cafes had always been gathering places for keen motorbikers, but café culture in the author's view properly began around 1956, thrived from 1958-on, boosted by the end of National Service in 1961, then peaked around 1962, tapering down to the well-publicised Mods'n'Rockers year of 1964, after which it tailed off as the Sixties proper and the counter-culture began to hold sway.

So the motorcycles described here, with the exception of the Vincent, run from 1957 to 1963-4. The aim is to provide a brief development history and character sketch of each of these iconic models, rather than an exhaustive year by year technical history. I am lucky enough to have ridden nearly all the machines in question while working as a classic bike journalist, and opinionated enough to have a view on all of them, which no doubt emerges from the text. The outstanding photographs illustrating each by my friend Garry Stuart should convey their power and appeal, and the riding shots show how they looked on the road when they were viewed as Menaces To Society.

With the exception of the Vincent and the pair of singles, all the bikes are 650 twins, except for the Royal Enfield Constellation – which is a 700 twin. Many of their specifications were broadly similar. But their differences were very important at the time! Dedicated café racers would tune and tweak their mounts for extra performance, as considered briefly in Chapter I.

But our business is with the raw material, the production motorcycles made by the British industry as it flared before fading.

HOW TO USE THIS BOOK

As usual with British motorcycles, the manufacturing year began anywhere from late August to, in a few cases, November; and ended in August. Thus when this book refers to "a 1958 Triumph" or "a Triumph for 1958," that machine might well have been built late in 1957, but its model year and specification were for 1958.

ABBREVIATIONS

AMC	Associated Motor Cycles
BDC	Bottom dead centre
BSA	Birmingham Small Arms
bhp	Brake horsepower
Imp.	Imperial: UK measurement, which differs from US
ISDT	International Six Day Trial
MIRA	Motor Industries Research Association, test track outside Nuneaton, Warks
ohc	overhead camshaft
ohv	overhead valve
rpm	revs per minute
sls	single leading shoe
TDC	Top dead centre
tls	twin leading shoe

ACKNOWLEDGEMENTS

First thanks must go to the unselfish owners of the beautiful motorcycles photographed in the book, who gave up their time to provide and to ride their cherished machines. In no particular order, they are: Rob Taylor (Constellation), Colin Austin (Rocket Gold Star), Peter Rosenthal (Gold Star), Rob Drury (Venom), Matthew Hilton (650SS), Jim Shed (Black Shadow Series C) and Chris Lucking (650CSR – and commiserations to Keith Lax, who had been more than willing, but then got knocked off his CSR!). Final thanks once again to Cliff and Kevin Rushworth at Ace Classics (T100/T110/T120).

For co-ordinating us with several of the above, thanks to my unstinting Editor James Robinson at *The Classic Motor Cycle*, a Mortons Motorcycle Media publication, and Mortons' archive supplied some of the background period photos, quickly and efficiently. Other helpful facilitators included Chris Read of the AJS/Matchless Owners Club, and John Thrussell. Useful information was provided by Les Emery at Fairspares, Roger Sharman of Cake Street Classics, by my former college mate Mike Sewell, and Mark Wilsmore at the Ace Café.

For printed sources, pride of place has to go to Mick Duckworth's amazingly comprehensive and enjoyable *Ace Times* (Red Line Publishing). Ray Knight's *Ever More Speed* (Lily Publications), and Bill Cakebread's *Motorcycle Apprentice* (Veloce) were also helpful sources; and an invaluable one was the second, unpublished half of the late Roland Pike's autobiography, which had been provided for me by Gold Star expert the late John Gardner, though I see it is now accessible on the Web.

Finally thanks to our publishers Charles and Ed Herridge for their fortitude and patience!

Steve Wilson, June 2014

CHAPTER 1:
THE ROCKER ROAD

"Too fast to live
Too young to die
When I do
No one will cry"

Too Fast To Live, *Robert Gordon*

Marlon Brando, a Rocker template, in 1953's The Wild One – even if the film was banned in Britain until 1968.

Brando deserved the UK ban because of that hat alone! And hang on, that's not a Triumph, it's a Moto Guzzi!

Time is a river, and as the wise man said, you can never step in the same river twice. A case in point was a seminal moment from The Wild One, a film from 1953 that for a generation helped to define the motorcyclist as rebel. In a small-town bar, a half-cut hairdresser's assistant, excited by the bikers who have taken over the place, fastens onto the "BRMC" legend on the back of their leather jackets, "Black Rebel Motorcycle Club". "Hey Johnny," she asks the leader of the pack, "what are you rebelling against?" And Marlon Brando slides his eyes the way he does, and says "What've you got?"

Well, what did they have, young men in the 1950s and early 60s? The legacy of World War and Holocaust, disrupted lives, broken homes and shattered economies, in Britain still exemplified by the city-centre bomb sites, unreconstructed over a decade after the Blitz, playgrounds for many of us where the fireweed bloomed. In this and other ways the war lingered on. In New Guinea, cargo cults grew up with

villagers fetishising the detritus left behind from the conflict. Half a world away the baby boom generation, with more boys than girls born as is usual in wartime, remained collectively obsessed by the fighter planes, battleships and armoured vehicles with which the vast battles had been waged. Tools to the men who used them, for the next generation they became icons from a last age of certainty. It was no coincidence that British motorcycles in the Sixties took the fighter planes' names – Spitfire, Hurricane, Lightning, Typhoon, Thunderbolt.

Till the mid-Fifties, cars and motorcycles were mostly finished in decently muted colours, black, dark green or maroon. Even after the austerity days, following prolonged wartime sacrifice, self-control, rationing and in-it-together, any kind of extravagance or unconventional behaviour continued to be strongly disapproved of. Respectability exercised a stranglehold. A progressively-minded doctor later told me of his Fifties' days as a GP in a new outer London suburb, and how much time he spent persuading its housewives to think outside the box, that for instance it was really all right for them to sometimes leave the house without a hat on. In 1961 my girlfriend at college had let her blonde hair grow a little, nothing extreme, just shoulder-length at most. Back at her suburban home in a provincial city for the Christmas holidays, she woke one night to find that her mother had crept into her bedroom and was hacking off her beautiful hair with pinking shears.

The older generation were used to obeying and to being obeyed. During the 1958 Notting Hill race riots, a police constable confronted a young man astride a motorcycle in company with about fifty white youths "dressed in Edwardian-type clothing. I told him to move," said PC Coe, "and he said 'Why the hell should I?'" Such open defiance of authority, which took place three or four miles from the legendary Ace café, caused resentment and outrage in the majority, especially after it had begun to be amplified by horror stories in the papers. The following incident was narrated to Mick Duckworth for *Ace Times* (Redline Books), his definitive, highly readable book on ton-up and Rocker culture and all its works. It was told to him by Bob Yerby, one of the fast Ace regulars.

"We were building up to near 100mph along the North Circular approaching the Pantiles [pub] when a van pulled out through a gap in the hedge between the carriageways. It was a short-cut to avoid the lights that people often used. The van went across to the left lane and we all had to take avoiding action. Tiny, who had Dave Lambert on the back, ran out of road and clipped the kerb. He hit his head on a lamp-post and Dave went over the top. I pulled up to help, but Dave died in my arms as I tried to get him off the road. A crowd was gathering and a woman said something I'll never forget: 'Good, that's another two of the bastards gone!'"

That was what we were rebelling against, and those were some of the responses we provoked. Emotional repression, outmoded attitudes and the "pettiness that plays so rough", those are the elements you can't reproduce today just by buying a retro-styled Hinckley Bonneville and a new £600 Lewis Leathers jacket.

None of this was quite new. Writing in 1928, D.H. Lawrence in Lady Chatterley's Lover has the Midlands working-class hero Mellors observe "The young [miners] scoot about on motor-bikes with girls, and jazz when they get the chance," though with the qualifier that "they're very dead. And it needs money…If you could only tell them that living and spending isn't the same thing." But industrialisation and materialism marched on.

World War 2 was at battlefield level an industrial conflict. For example, the vastly superior German Tiger and King Tiger tanks, which could literally blow the doors off the Allied opposition, nevertheless suffered from being such a quality, complex design that they could not be built in sufficient numbers to resist eventually being overwhelmed by waves of the cruder Sherman and T34 tanks churned out from the factories of the USA and USSR.

The British motorcycle factories which supplied the bulk of the machines for the Forces – BSA, Matchless and Norton, with to a lesser extent Royal Enfield, Triumph and Ariel – made profits from that so that they began the post-war period with a head start (though AJS/Matchless would dissipate theirs by spending the money on racing). In at least one case, the swords of war were almost literally beaten into ploughshares – at BSA, just after the war, Val Page and Herbert Perkins adapted redundant gun-barrel machinery to manufacture Page's new design of telescopic front fork. Tellingly, this fork then continued to be produced, largely unmodified, until 1971. The lack of investment in new tooling and designs which this example demonstrated would do for our industry shortly after that.

As with the car industry, decline, "snatched from the jaws of victory", sprang from a complex set of problems, which included successive governments' stop-go economic policies; inappropriate market strategies; and as with the aircraft industry, too many small firms duplicating effort and fragmenting the market. But at base, across the board there was a rigidity, an institutionalisation which became accepted as the norm, and which shaped the actions of the corporate players, leaving them incapable of adapting to an ever-changing world. The motoring industry

"We busted out of class,
had to get away from those fools
We learned more from a three minute record
than we ever did in school"

No Surrender, *Bruce Springsteen*

Home-grown. Partially Press-staged photo from 1964 Mods-and-Rockers Bank Holiday troubles.

historian Timothy R. Whisler calls this "path-dependence", and points out how such institutions act as filters for information, so that choices are based on imperfect knowledge.

Thus the disastrous AJS/Matchless boss Donald Heather could declare that motorcyclists enjoyed spending their weekends de-coking cylinder heads, at a time in the Fifties when the sale of motor scooters, almost all Continental imports, was well on the way to outstripping sales of motorcycles in the UK. The industry, eyes on the rear-view mirror, could only remember cautiously a brief scooter boom-and-bust after the First World War. But the new Italian and then German scooters not only needed little work on their efficiently designed, simple two-stroke engines, but the majority of their owners, who thanks to a scooter's layout could be male or female and could dress normally, didn't even want to see the engines beneath the colourful panelling, let alone de-coke them; and the importers set up efficient after-sales service networks to take care of that.

So Heather and others had been wrong about a major market segment, because they lived in an institutional matrix which shaped their decisions about what was possible, along with their fellow directors, many of them former competitors, from the same older genera-

WILDEST ONES

Mods wield deckchairs. Two leather-jacketed Rockers jump 15ft. to safety. This happened yesterday at Brighton.

Fight them on the beaches? Triumph twins were the Rockers' tool of choice.

tion as themselves, and their dealers, often successful ex-racers. As with most of the rest of the industry, this meant that their efforts were skewed in favour of competition-type machinery, by definition fast, large-capacity, noisy, oily and potentially dangerous. From within that path, this looked like simply the right stuff for healthily virile, competitive, mechanically competent young men. This obscured the fact that from outside it looked like anti-social anathema, especially after the rebel factor had reared its head.

"Nitor", columnist on The Motor Cycle, defined a yob in 1957 as "any young man who is brash, loudly ignorant, something of a nitwittish show-off." He had met many on the road over the Easter holiday. "Dropped handlebars, a racing crouch, facemasks, de-gutted silencers… are becoming far too common."

The Rockers of the Ton-up era bought into that whole ethos. Speed was their god, their heroes were racers, comfort and even durability came second to the last ounce of power, and they favoured big, powerful machinery. British machinery, naturally, for though this may have been the early post-Imperial period, popular faith in national superiority ran on, and especially in the world of speed. Donald Campbell broke the World Speed record on water, as Triumph motorcycles did (though it was disputed on

How the industry, in this case AMC's Matchless marque, saw potential customers in 1959…

…and how some of them actually were.

Rocker girl riders were a minority, but an eye-catching one.

The Café was a broad church: cowhorn bars on an early Bonneville contrast with clip-ons for the Beeza.

many were competent mechanically and some highly skilled. Unlike with today's restorers, there was no reverence for factory originality – we'll look at typical café racer conversions later – or even for the machines themselves: the burn-up was the thing. One Ace regular described "taking a bike like a Bonnie and riding it to its limit, the silencers all smashed in and the footrests all bent up: [that was] the satisfaction."

Thus the industry's "path-dependence" affected the motorcycling culture of the Fifties and early Sixties. So did other immediate social factors. Post-war, new factories were built outside towns, in places with good access to major roads, while new housing estates also were often sited on the edges of bombed-out towns and cities, and the absence of by-passes caused heavy traffic in towns themselves. This meant longer journeys to work for the fully employed workforce, on packed public transport which frequently failed to serve the new estates.

The growth of personal transport became a necessity, and where pre-war mobility had been revolutionised by the mass-produced bicycle, the greater commuting distances, as well as returning service-men and -women's familiarity with machinery, created fertile ground for the expansion of powered two-wheelers (PTWs), further encouraged by reasonable wages and a period of low inflation. With car ownership still out of reach for many, in the Fifties 3% of the UK's population rode to work on a PTW, which translated into 1.76 million two-wheelers on the road by 1960.

Britain until 1953 was the largest motorcycle manufacturer in the world. For 1950 it produced 180,000 motorcycles, but in the age of "Export or Die", sent 74,000 of them abroad. At the same time, as mentioned, the "path-dependent" industry missed out on a major segment of the market. Though production and sales would rise throughout the Fifties, to a peak in 1959 of 331,806 new machines, that was a sales figure, and 65% of it was for machines of 150cc or less, the vast majority of them imported German mopeds and Italian scooters. The UK's only numerically significant home-produced lightweight in the period had been BSA's Bantam, with around half a million built by the end in 1971; and that had been derived from a German DKW design seized as war reparation. Our own scooters were often motorcycle-oriented (chain driven, with separate frames and tubular silencers) and too little, too late. As the scooter boom waned at the end of the Fifties, following the lifting of trade restrictions with Japan in 1960, Honda's C100 Super-Cub would arrive to provide the answer, reliable, lightweight and unthreatening, to the utility two-wheel question, and

a technicality) for two wheels on land, in 1956 at Bonneville salt flats. Mike Hawthorn was the World Champion race driver for 1958, Stirling Moss won the Italian Grand Prix, and while Italian multi-cylinder racing motorcycles displaced even Featherbed-framed Manx Nortons as GP track winners, their top riders – Geoff Duke for Gilera, with Mike Hailwood and John Surtees for the last players, MV Agusta – were often British. Commercially, the industry still effectively excluded alternative big bike roadsters from BMW and Harley-Davidson with swingeing import duties. So the Rockers' machines of choice came from BSA, Norton and Triumph.

These high-powered motorcycles needed frequent mechanical attention to keep running and give of their best. Lack of money and relatively simple designs meant that Rockers provided that attention amongst themselves, hands-on by definition. This was accepted – "If they don't break, how're you going to learn to fix 'em?" There was the inevitable quota of bodgers, but sell in millions worldwide.

The economic exhaustion caused by the war and the need to redress the balance of payments (that "Export or Die"), also helped to stifle necessary investment in new plant and designs for the motorcycle industry, while high demand both at home and in a still-captive colonial market masked that situation. So did the brilliant efforts of often maverick individuals, usually at odds with their bosses, who improved what already existed, with developments like Norton's Featherbed frame and BSA's great sporting all-rounder, the Gold Star. As with the aircraft industry (The Comet! The Vulcan!), Britain could still appear to be on top.

But as one man crucial to the Gold Star's evolution, the Irish off-road star and talented engineer Bill Nicholson, put it, "The entire industry, and not just BSA, were completely blinded after the war by the demand for bikes. They thought the boom would never end. Anything and everything was built and sold, and there was some real rubbish produced! There was no development, nothing new, nothing planned and set aside for the future. It had to fail."

Flames, however, often burn brightest before they burn out, and in this brief intervening period Britain was producing the fastest street motorcycles in the world.

Meanwhile the problem remained for young working-class men, as it had for Lawrence's miners: what might masculinity consist of in this curious age? Rockers were an almost exclusively working-class phenomenon, like motorcycling in general; as indicated by the fact that while 25% of cars were purchased on Hire Purchase (aka "the Drip", or "the Never-Never", and a prime weapon in managing that government Stop-Go policy), the figure was 75% for two-wheelers. The monotony and frustration of day-long factory work provided the impetus to discover the freedom a motorbike offered, and then get together with mates and dice with death on the night roads.

Arthur Seaton, the young working-class hero of Alan Sillitoe's 1958 novel *Saturday Night and Sunday Morning*, at a lathe in the Raleigh works at Nottingham, "experienced…the factory smell of oil-suds, machinery and shaved steel that surrounded you with an air in which pimples grew and prospered on your face…What a life he thought, hard work and good wages and a smell all day that turns your guts… machines…belts over my head…slapping and twisting and thumping… a noise that made your brain reel and ache…it's a hard life if you don't weaken." (The antiquated belt-driven machinery featured widely in the motorcycle industry, even in

Talking bikes outside the all-night Ace Café.

"*Gee Officer Krupke, we're down on our knees, Cos no one wants a feller with a social disease*"

Gee, Officer Krupke!, *West Side Story*

In the late Fifties, working class rebellion over the boredom of repetitive industrial labour was not confined to Rockers.

Outside the Ace with a Gold Star-styled BSA twin.

Triumph-mounted mates. Was the Ban-the-Bomb symbol from political conviction or for maximum outrage?

Triumph's new works at Meriden, had been salvaged from their bombed-out factory in Coventry.) As Arthur memorably put it in the film version, "Nine hundred and fifty four, nine hundred and fifty bloody five. Another few more and that's the lot for a Friday."

It was a time overshadowed by the memories and heroes of the recently won war, yet living in dread of a coming nuclear conflict; and also a time so tired and disenchanted with war that when a call-up for other-

ranks reservists came with the Korean crisis, enough men simply ignored it for the government to decide not to pursue them. This was an age of bombed-out city centres yet decent wages and paid holidays, of frequently crowded housing with inadequate sanitation, but with the time to enjoy the better health, increased leisure and mass consumption as promoted by "the haunted fish-tank" in the corner, the TV increasingly becoming a fixture in Britain's homes

Conflicted identity? Author in the mid-Sixties. Bronx jacket and Converse sneakers, but Norton 88 De-Luxe panelled like a scooter, and is that haircut a bit Mod?

Talented Ron Wittich, with Jenny, went racing.

through the Fifties.

But for young people it hadn't yet ousted the cinema as what sociological jargon mangled into "a central site for identity formation", and post-war the cinema, despite Ealing comedies, was primarily a vehicle for the colonisation of our unconscious by the USA, the American Way up there in Technicolor and Cinemascope. The Wild One might be banned in the UK, but Blackboard Jungle, Rebel Without A Cause and The Young Savages, as well as West Side Story on stage and LP, got the flick-knife-and-leather-jacket gospel across. We looked and learned.

By 1959, there were five million teenagers in the UK, with £800 million to spend annually. The mainstream young might be discovering frothy cappuccinos, dispensed by an explosive Gaggia machine and drunk from clear glass cups and saucers while sitting on cane chairs surrounded by rubber plants, with jazz on the jukebox. But a caff was not a coffee bar; the only thing the bad boys shared with that scenario was the jukebox, and in the cafés what it played was mostly rock'n'roll. Not always to everybody's taste; John Lennon and the boys in pre-Beatles days were said to have been thrown out of the Ace for feeding the box incessant shillings (three records for a shilling) and playing nothing but a single Buddy Holly track, over and over. There was even a blank record, three minutes' silence for the terminally disenchanted. But in a relatively brief period from 1956 to early 1959, the rebel souls knew they had their soundtrack. Kiss-curled and chubby Bill Haley was more for the Teds, the foot-soldiers. Elvis, Little Richard, Buddy Holly, Jerry Lee Lewis, Gene Vincent and Chuck Berry were the men, the real joyous and explosive deal. The leather boys weren't called Rockers because of their bikes' valve gear, though there was a nice ambivalence there.

The motorcycle connection with rock'n'roll music was always there. In Mississippi Elvis kept a pack of Harleys for self and friends. In Texas, Holly and the Crickets, dissed at the Harley dealers, bought big Triumphs and an Ariel 650 Cyclone. Gene "Be-Bop-A-Lula" Vincent's distinctive limp came from crashing his new Triumph during his US military service, and his stage outfit was black leathers; on UK tours he was an Ace aficionado, along with home-grown Johnny Kidd and the Pirates from nearby Willesden. As the musical tide flowed over the Atlantic, the diminutive Adam Faith from Acton was an all-night Ace regular in Cuban heels after the Soho coffee bars had closed, on a T110 with shortened rear shocks to suit his stature. Cliff Richard, initially a rocking singer, who officially opened the original motorcycle-oriented Church youth outfit, the 59 Club, played a juvenile delinquent's

Rocker girl on late BSA A10 modified with alloy guards, clip-ons and separate Goldie-style headlamp.

younger brother in his first film, Serious Charge. But "Move It!" gave way to "Living Doll", and Adam Faith's "What Do You Want?" mined the cheesier latter days of Buddy Holly, as Buddy died, Elvis went into the US Army, "Teen-beat" took over the charts and the music went to sleep for the next four years.

Parents thought the Rockers and their music were

Adam Faith mounts his Bonneville in 1960 film, Never Let Go.

> *"In the empty Houston streets of four o'clock in the morning a motorcycle kid suddenly roared through…slick black jacket, a Texas poet of the night, girl gripped on his back like a papoose, hair flying… They pin-pointed out of sight."*

On The Road, *Jack Kerouac*

"Spiritual dry rot? Nah mate, don't get a lot of that round 'ere."

as dandified and effeminate as their Brylcreemed pompadour coiffes, and as menacing, like the high jackboots and silver-studded black jackets with their unpleasant echoes of Wehrmacht tank crews and the Waffen SS – so that was a double result in the boys' age-old struggle to differentiate themselves from their fathers. As with D.H. Lawrence, post-war intellectuals like Richard Hoggart disapproved in a different way, writing in 1957 that "the jukebox boys" had "spiritual dry-rot". There may have been a post-war vacuum morally – Sillitoe's Arthur Seaton says "What I'm out for is a good time – all the rest is propaganda" – but getting away from the judgemental gaze of parents and neighbours was one big reason to go to the caffs.

Jenny Wittich on lowered Triumph-engined special.

As with the music, the evolution of the Rockers' weapons of choice, mostly large-capacity parallel twins, was decisively affected by influences from the other side of the Atlantic, and nowhere more so than at Triumph. Their boss Edward Turner was an instinctively skilled predictor of market trends; he didn't always get it right, but he frequently went against the British motorcycle industry's institutionalised ideas, and headed its most successful company. Even before the war he had seen the potential for his trend-setting Speed Twin and Tiger 100 machines in the USA, a place he liked. Paradoxically, at home he aimed to produce motorcycles with the opposite qualities to the ones prized by young Americans: bikes that were quiet, smooth and with consciously graceful, almost delicate styling. Also, unlike Matchless and Norton, Turner at Triumph, despite having raced himself in the Twenties, firmly discouraged factory-backed racing as unprofitable.

Further, to tap into the mass commuter market, he aimed to produce "Everyman" machines, light, low and, like scooters, featuring as much panelling as possible, which could be finished in bright, often two-tone colours and which aimed to protect the rider from road dirt and to be easy to clean. This was progressive thinking but it largely fell flat, particularly in America. (He also designed a couple of actual scooters, but one was a heavyweight only released for 1958 after that trend had peaked, and the other an automatic anticipating today's twist'n'go, but under-gunned at 100cc, bedevilled with teething problems, and again, in 1961, too late against the Japanese.)

The Americans had other ideas. Since mass-produced cheap automobiles had long ago undercut motorcycle prices, and the vast distances and Inter-state freeway network made travel virtually the preserve of four wheels and more, so motorcycles became all about leisure and sport. Triumph's US distributors saw their sales benefit from winning on the dirt-track ovals, in enduros and latterly on tarmac, and with higher-octane gasoline available and cheap, they designed and produced sporting and tuning goodies for the British twins. Turner himself at least bowed to American demands for more powerful road-sters; having built the first commercially successful 500cc parallel twin, for 1949 he deftly expanded it into the first 650. BSA had caught wind of this and did likewise, and the other manufacturers eventually followed suit.

There was direct American influence when the men from Triumph's East and West Coast distributors' development departments visited Meriden, where they surreptitiously passed hot pistons, camshafts and valve springs to Henry Vale of Triumph UK's tiny

"But cheap greasy meals
Are hardly a
home on the range"

Captain Fantastic and the Brown Dirt Cowboy,
Elton John

Competition Department, which was mostly concerned with scramblers and with twins for the ISDT. The result began to appear on the sports roadster twins, the 500cc Tiger 100 and 650 Tiger 110, from 1954, when they also first adopted a swinging-arm frame. The effect on the café scene was immediate. "Up to around 1954 to '55," said Bob Innes, Ace regular and builder of Triumph-engined racing specials, "in the flying jacket era, not black leather, the majority of fast bikes had been retired racers – AJS 7Rs, Mk VIII cammy Velos, single cam Manx Nortons," (all singles, and he could have included pre-war Ariel Red Hunters tuned to run on methanol, and post-war Douglas sports twins like the 90 Plus). "Then the Triumph started becoming the thing. They were reasonably cheap, you could get the spares, and they could be tuned – and they certainly had the mystique. Triumphs were the most popular." The other manufacturers, as you will read, caught up, sooner or later, but their products were less numerous, and both their machines and the tuning parts were more expensive. For Rockers, despite their drawbacks, Triumphs ruled.

The café racer scene, like real rock'n'roll, was quite defined in its time period, and divided by the moment at the beginning of 1961 when the media spotlight focussed on the Rockers, first via an episode of Dixon of Dock Green with scenes filmed on location at the Ace and featuring record racing (Bob Innes: "In all the years I was going down the Ace, from before '52 till it closed in '69, I never ever saw that, a record race.") A few weeks later, the Daily Mirror hit its 14 million readers with the "SUICIDE CLUB!" edition, the 6-page cover story written by now-legendary campaigning Left journalist John Pilger. Its central motif was the ever-increasing casualty figure among two-wheelers. In 1959, 1680 riders had been killed and 128,614 injured. This had represented half of that year's road casualties, when only a fifth of vehicles had been two-wheeled. And an alarming proportion of the dead or injured riders had been youngsters.

Excited by the prospect of being bona fide Menaces To Society, leather boys flocked to the Ace and, by jeering and throwing things at passing motorists and the police, drew the first full-on raid at the café the night after the *Mirror* story appeared, with 20

arrested. From then on the police were more pro-active on the local roads, and later in 1961 Parliament passed the Hughes-Hallett Act, limiting Learner riders to machines of 250cc or less.

Previously at the Ace, in an instinctively British hierarchical arrangement, the hard core of the fastest riders had sat at the two tables closest to the entrance, with their bikes parked nearest the door outside. That was lads like "Noddy" Barry Chase, the King of the Ace, and skilled specials builder Ron Wittich, who went on to ride production racers for Gus Kuhn, and would die on the track in 1972. They were nightly regulars, not just weekenders or drop-ins on Thursday, the big night when Wembley Stadium a mile away hosted Speedway, with crowds of up to 85,000 (it was then the second biggest spectator sport in England).

Duckworth's book quotes from a 1963 article in a student magazine by Alan Hendry (600 Norton, Triumph Bonneville), a regular Ace visitor who noted that "most [of the fastest riders] had been engineering

*February 1961
Daily Mirror shock-
horror story led to
crack-down on speeding
Rockers and the Ace.*

*Sometimes you run
out of road.*

apprentices or motor mechanics, and by then the type seemed to be disappearing"; also that the Ace was quieter than in '59 because of the police attention.

Rockers would come in for another burst of negative media attention in 1964, with the Mods v. Rockers seaside battles, but that was very much a Press creation. Up till then motorbike riders and scooterists largely co-existed amicably. Even in 1965 when I was stuck with a punctured Norton on the A21 Hastings road, and a vanload of Mods pulled up on their way to Camber Sands, they cheerfully loaded up the Norton and took me to Camier's bike shop in Rye. Duckworth quotes a Mod who grew up on a London estate where "It never occurred to me to beat Rockers up; they used to help us fix our scooters."

Harry Winch, a leather-jacketed AMC 650CSR rider from south-east London, recalled one trip taken in a Thames van to a south coast town in company with a load of Mods. When they got there, newspaper photographers followed the mixed group about, waiting for trouble, and in the end one of the snappers offered them money to start something. "He was sent away with some choice remarks," said Harry. "As far as I was concerned, the scooter contingent were on two wheels like everybody else." But tribal warfare made a better story, and young people bought into it: "Buttons", future President of the UK Hells Angels, grew up as a leather boy in the East End, and found that in 1964/5, "The Mods were our automatic enemies and we were theirs. Why it came about, I

don't know." After regular brawling, Buttons ended up near to death after a Mod put a shotgun round in his chest at close range one night on Hackney Mare Street.

In Harry Winch's view, "From 1958 to 1962 was the true age of the coffee-bar cowboy." I would only add a prequel from 1955 and a coda to 1964. It was a country-wide phenomenon, but the Ace was the mecca at the centre of a loose web of cafés around London, prominent ones including the Busy Bee eight miles away on the Watford by-pass where the M1 now ends, Johnson's on the A20 by Brands Hatch circuit, and the Tip-Top on the Kingston by-pass. The Ace stood out with its neon signage, glass frontage and clock tower on the old North Circular, a genuine modern transport café with petrol pumps, a shirt-and-tie restaurant for the drivers, upstairs accommodation and one of the first automatic car washes. The Ace was open 24 hours a day, so when other cafés like the Dug-Out at Golders Green or the Cellar in Windsor turned out, Rockers could ride/race to the Ace.

Fellow night-hawks there included the music crowd down from Soho, but otherwise there was little glamour about the smoke-filled main room with its tired truckers, bookies' runners, ladies of the night who mocked the young riders often fresh out of school, petty criminals and undercover police earwigging "fallen-off-a-lorry" transactions, connecting with their informants and keeping an eye out for teenage runaway girls. This was marginal, the edges of society. The very large car park for the wagons was often littered with broken glass and slick with oil and diesel spill, which unhorsed many riders making the obligatory feet-up, high-speed entrance. Thefts of parts, or of whole bikes belonging to riders who arrived from outside, were not unknown. And the food was better at the Busy Bee.

Among the bikers there were some genuine oddballs and outsiders. Bob Innes recalled "Tiddler Humphreys – he was a character – he rode an all-chromed Triumph and he never seemed to have a job that was normal. He'd just got sacked as an undertaker and I found him one night in the Ace reading a book. 'It's for me new job,' he said – it was a manual on how to hang someone. He'd become assistant to Pierrepoint" (the UK's most famous executioner). "Tiddler rode in Speedway, for Hackney I think, under the name of Tyburn Gallows. One match they built an effigy of the opposing skipper and strung it up, with Tiddler as the hangman. It was in the papers, and when the Home Office got to hear about it somehow, he lost that job too…"

But there could be magic at the Ace, a buzz, and a lot of laughter and camaraderie among the young riders sitting on the low wall outside, watching the scene. They usually didn't drink or smoke, as every hard-earned penny went on their machines and petrol. There was a minority of leather girl pillion passengers, often fearful their parents would find out, and an even smaller number of female riders. There was plenty of horseplay ("Noddy" connecting the bolted-down Bel Ami jukebox by the door to a lorry about to pull away) but surprisingly little violence, especially after "Tex" Childs, a large ABA boxer, took over as night manager following a rare incident during which the current manager had legged it. "My mate Keith was joking with someone," Tex told me, "using rough language, and this nasty little red-headed Scots bloke thought it was aimed at him and went for him with a broken ketchup bottle. It was bad, he cut Keith's little finger tendon through at the wrist. We sat on the Scot hard."

Trying for ton-plus runs past the Ace's frontage on the 40mph dual-carriageway was popular, and so was racing in groups to or from the Busy Bee, last one in buying the coffee. At Johnson's on the A20, known as Joe's, a rapid 15-mile run went down the Mad Mile straight from Sidcup, under the narrow railway arches and past the Dutch House pub at Eltham, where speed groupie girls waited on the wall for a fast ride; or up Gorse Hill, the three-lane section by Brands Hatch circuit itself, which became known as Death Hill due

> *"Well I'd sooner forget,*
> *but I remember those nights*
> *When life was just a bet*
> *on a race between*
> *the lights"*
>
> **Telegraph Road**, *Dire Straits*

to the wipe-out rate for motorcyclists.

Some of the Johnson's crowd were on the rough side; veteran sprinter Frank Clarke told *Classic Bike* recently how they would bang six-inch nails into their boots to run up the side of cars that had cut them up. The "King of Johnson's", John Letchford or J.L., along with future journalist Charlie Rous on a Vincent twin, was one of a number of fast boys out of that venue – though further down the A20 at the bottom of Wrotham Hill, the Oakdene café mob, which in the mid-Fifties included future racer and premier frame-builder Colin Seeley, "thought we were a cut above the Johnson's lot…rockers and posers…and had more riding skills on our faster bikes, so would often show off as we raced home from the Oakdene to the Farningham roundabout, when flat on the tank a derogatory hand signal might be given to the sad lot

Production racing was an important part of the scene. Here a lone Triumph Tiger 100 passes a café, contesting the 1955 IoM 500 Clubmans TT – already a BSA Gold Star benefit.

*Typical, smart Triton – pre-
unit 650 Triumph engine in
Norton Featherbed frame,
with big 4ls front brake and
race styling*

Typical, smart Triton – pre-unit 650 Triumph engine in Norton Featherbed frame, with big 4ls front brake and race styling

Another take on the Triton.

outside Johnson's." But later there was nothing sad about J.L., who ran a very, very stripped-down Bonneville in a lightweight special frame, said to be good for over 120mph.

That was the point with real Rockers, to get hold of a fast machine like the ones in this book, and then make it even faster. More than that, as Mike Clay spelt out in his book *Café Racers*, from the mid-Fifties relative teenage prosperity meant that their motorbikes

could become not just something to ride, but status symbols. And status symbols by definition had to look impressive – which in this case meant looking fast.

The most obvious and universal go-faster badges were race-style, dropped, preferably "clip-on" handlebars – which Triumph's shapely nacelle headlamp and its imitators, Royal Enfield's casquette and the two BSA versions of headlamp cowl, made tricky if not impossible to fit. Dropped "Ace" bars were a compromise, even when they featured alloy ball-ended control levers. Separate headlamp shells on separate mounts, as finally found on the 1960 T120 Bonneville, were what was needed, and they also allowed the desired jutting twinned instruments, speedo and rev counter, on alloy mounts. On the street, headlamps were often removed altogether, with feeble bicycle lights substituted as a sop to the law. "We thought it was fun to strip off the lights like a racer," said Bob Innes. "I stole so many of my mum's frying pans, cut the handles off and they'd look like Manx racing number plates, to us at any rate. Then we'd put a cycle lamp on and go down the Watford by-pass at night, three lanes with a suicide lane in the middle, you couldn't see much and the only way to keep going was to find the cat's eyes, drrt, drrt, drrt as you rode over them and you knew you were OK."

Skinny alloy mudguards replaced the standard,

often heavily valanced, painted steel ones, while front fork springs were either exposed or covered by rubber gaiters. Front brakes might be embellished with alloy "bacon-slicer" cooling discs, or four-leading-shoe racing brakes from Fontana substituted. Steel wheel rims were swapped for alloy ones. Petrol tanks were junked in favour of race-style ones, both bigger and lighter, in alloy or fibreglass. Rear-set footrests and controls were mounted above the replacement swept-back exhaust pipes, sometimes siamesed, and ending in one or two truncated, megaphone, or sometimes even empty silencers, the Clubmans Gold Star style being a favourite. Leopardskin print seat covers, or better yet a racing seat with a rear hump, were possible further additions. The common factor was "added lightness" and the subliminal message was racer style. The other must-have feature was twin carbs. They were fiddly to set up and keep in tune, and on their own added little or nothing at the top end, but to your peer group their presence said you were serious about speed.

Mechanically, higher compression pistons, GP

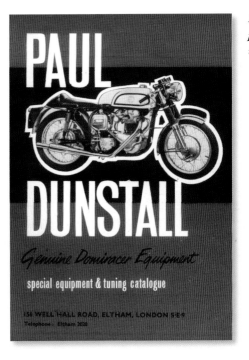

Paul Dunstall became the top purveyor of café racer components, as well as complete Production racers.

A choice of Dunstall goodies.

PETROL TANKS

5-GALLON RACING PATTERN

This glassfibre petrol tank is finished in the Norton colours of silver with a black and red line and is supplied complete with transfer. Fitted with a Monza quick action filler cap, it is suitable only for use with the racing seat. Price £13.0.0. complete. 3½ gallon tank has a similar appearance and finish for use with normal dual seat £11.10.0.

NEW!
LOWLINE TANK

This is the very latest pattern 3½ gallon glassfibre streamlined tank, finished in silver with black and red lining and fitted with a Monza filler cap. For use with racing seat only. £8.10.0. each.

CENTRAL OIL TANK

Glassfibre central oil tank similar to Manx pattern finished in Norton colours of silver with black and red lining. Complete with Monza cap, £9.0.0.

DOMIRACER SEAT

This is a replica of the Domiracer seat and will fit all featherbed framed models. Made from glassfibre covered with good quality rexine. £4.10.0. Please state model and year when ordering. Domiracer dual seat, £5.10.0.

Huge Stocks of Ordinary Dominator Spare Parts Always Available
All items can be supplied C.O.D. or cash with order

POST AND PACKING CHARGES ARE AS FOLLOWS:
UP TO £1 VALUE .. 2/0d.
£1—£4 VALUE .. 2/6d.
£4—£8 VALUE .. 4/0d.
Over £8 VALUE.. 6/0d.

CALL WRITE OR PHONE 9 am—6 pm MONDAY to SATURDAY (except Thursday closed all day)

DOUBLE SPEED OIL PUMP

This double speed oil pump conversion is accurately made from good quality steel and is a must for the really hard rider, £2.10.0. each. Sports special large capacity oil pump £5.8.0. complete.

PISTONS

All pistons are supplied in pairs complete with rings, gudgeon pins and circlips. Bore sizes available: standard, plus .020 in., plus .030 in., plus .040 in. and plus .060 in.

Pre 1962 Norton 88, 9 : 1 standard, £8.12.0, oversize, £8.18.0.
Post 1962 Norton 88 9.75 : 1, standard, £8.12.0, oversize, £8.18.0.
Pre 1962 Norton 99, 9.0 : 1, standard, £5.15.0, oversize, £7.4.0.
Post 1962 Norton 99, 9.75 : 1, standard, £6.15.0, oversize, £7.4.0.
All Norton 650 S.S, 10.5 : 1, standard and oversize, £9.0.0.
All Norton Atlas 750, 9.0 : 1, standard and oversize, £9.0.0.

Compression plates for models 88, 99 and 650 .010 in. and .020 in. thick, 10/- each. Please state model and year when ordering.

ENGINE SPROCKETS

A full range of engine sprockets is available for Norton 88, 99, 650 and 750 models. 17-19 teeth £1.15.0. each; 20-23 teeth £1.17.6. each; 24-25 teeth £2.0.0. each. Close ratio gear cluster complete to fit AMC gearbox £23.10.0.

SPECIAL TIMING COVER

This special timing cover replaces the existing one to enable you to fit the rev counter drive. Highly polished alloy casting £4.6.0. Camshaft end nut to drive rev counter 9/6d. each. Rev counter gear box drive £2.7.6. Rev counter cable 17/6d. Rev counter instrument head £5.0.0. Mounting bracket for rev counter head 19/6d. Competition magneto £18.6.0. Sprocket for manual control magneto £1.7.6. Sprocket for automatic magneto £3.0.6.

The ultimate improvement was the Triton, a machine built up by slotting a (usually) pre-unit Triumph engine into a (normally) Norton Wideline Featherbed frame, so that the most tuneable twin was married to the ultimate in race-bred good handling. "[Dealer and tuner] Geoff Monty's Manx with a Triumph engine in it was the first Triton I knew about," said Bob Innes. "Then Daphne Amott at Geoff Amott's built the Manx-engined Formula 3 race cars, and they had a pen with five or six Manx Norton rolling chassis parked in it, for sale at £150 each. That was a lot of money" (a complete new Triumph T110 cost around £240 in the mid-Fifties) "but they were genuine Manx. That started the Triton thing."

Honed and tuned machines from the Ace, usually after midnight when in the earlier days the police patrols had gone home, were then hurled at the ultimate 3½-mile there-and-back street race, with or without a three-minute record on the Bel-Ami jukebox to beat. Blast left out of the car park, roar northward up the North Circular under the railway arches, shoot the Stonebridge lights if you had to, throttle up to a three-quarter-mile 90mph right-hand sweeper, then take the climbing left-hander to the treacherous girders of the Iron Bridge – there had been a ridge in the road where riders of rigid machines used to get nearly thrown off – which had to be exited at no less than 80mph. Then it was brake to 65 for a downhill left-hander, and finally a quarter-mile right-hander to the Neasden roundabout, tear round with everything scraping and sparking on the asphalt, then run the same route in reverse to rocket home.

It had to be done at the limit, and either bad luck or lack of skill could prove fatal. Rocker Paul Evison, also known as Heinrich von Tritonhausen, told Mike Clay how he was passed one night by some riders racing along that way from the Ace to the Bee, and then in the distance saw their tail-lights abruptly jump high in the air. An articulated lorry had pulled out of a side-turning. On the scene Evison vividly recalled one pretty young girl pillion lying by the road, unmarked but stone dead. It seems that another female pillion also died, while the riders survived. Over one fortnight, seven motorcyclists were killed at the Iron Bridge alone. Late 1964. "It was a depressed era for biking. The clip-on and rear-sets brigade were fading away…the racing crouch was hard work for squirting around London – and the leather jacket image was taking a bashing. Flashed-up scooters were everywhere. There were never any rockers. The scene

Jenny, Ron Wittich's partner, outside the Ace with the 200cc Tiger Cub her parents bought her for her 16th birthday. In fact the Cub embarrassed her – as the boys had taught her to ride faster bikes some time before…

carbs, Morgo replacement oil pumps for Triumphs along with the same firm's big-bore conversions for them, or alloy cylinder barrels from ARE, were all bolt-on options. After that, in the Sixties you could resort to specialists like Paul Dunstall, a former Johnson's rider, for lowered Featherbed-framed specials as well as bolt-on goodies, John Tickle also for goodies including improved front brakes, or Taylor Dow for a full range of Gold Star and BSA twin uprates, notably "Superleggera" front forks with two-way damping. Rockers' machines could end up as individualised as their leather jackets did after studs, chains, badges and paint jobs had been added.

"Rebels Don't Ride Japanese"

Ian Glover-James

simply moved fast in about two years and bikers stood still. They got labelled."

Soon after that, however, 6pm to 2am police patrols were instituted, now equipped with the 100mph 650 Triumph "Saint" machines, as well as some 125mph V8 Daimler Dart cars. Up till then chases with the police had generated an element of grudging admiration from the Traffic men for some of the Ace riders' skill, plus an unwillingness to prosecute if it meant admitting they had been out-run. (Elsewhere it wasn't always that cosy – sprinter Frank Clarke one night on a race to the Dutch House clipped the handlebars of a slow-moving sidecar outfit with his ohc International Norton. "I didn't realise, but the police had seen me and were in hot pursuit. They couldn't keep up with me though; the first I knew of it was having my face slammed into the tiles as I was using the pub toilet. I was handcuffed and dragged across the car park, under arrest for dangerous driving at 100mph.") In West London in 1961, with Press and public outrage high, orders from above to charge all offenders were now strictly carried out; there was then no upper speed limit on the open road, but if you were booked for "driving at a speed dangerous to the public", it meant an instant loss of licence – and magistrates would never question the word of the police.

Inadequate drum brakes, hard low-hysteresis rubber for tyres, poor lights, and rising speeds which overwhelmed chassis designed for the country's winding cart-track and Roman-road based highways all contributed to the Rockers' risk. There was also the changing character of the riders as, after the publicity, new youngsters flocked to the cafés, with sometimes, police estimated, up to a thousand bikes a night at the Ace. As Ron Wittich's widow Jenny told Duckworth, "Ron always said that he only took calculated risks and that once you made a decision on the road you shouldn't hesitate. All our group thought about the risks, but I think some of the younger ones coming into it in the Sixties just took chances, without calculating."

So why did they do it? Perhaps you have to imagine being young again, 18, after a week of mind-numbingly repetitive work, doing what you were told by grey older men, how it felt to slice through the night beside your mates, at full noise, draped in a racing crouch astride a powerful machine you'd built up yourself and knew through and through. Then the deep roar rises when you twist the throttle another inch, and feel the rear end squirm heart-stoppingly – but don't back off! – as you lay the plot hard into a damp, slick, sweeping left-hander, sparks flying vividly as centre-stands and silencers scrape and ground, jink past a suddenly-looming slow car faster than thought, never backing

off a fraction, easing inch by inch ahead of the pack, vibration making the twin a living thing beneath you, everything else excluded in the total concentration as your watering eyes strain to read the ill-lit road and the flickering speedo, but still ahead, still King of the bloody Road. Get it wrong and you'll end up in hospital or the morgue. Get it right and stay lucky, and there'll never be another feeling like it.

For the majority, this was a fleeting phase in their lives. Some died; a few, waking up to the random risk on the road or the prospect of trouble with the law, channelled their skill and passion onto the track – from the Ace came Ray Pickrell, Dave Degens and Dave "Crasher" Croxford. But for most, it was marriage and a family. And the times moved on too. The first miles of motorway had come late in 1958, signalling a shift from the Tory's previous long-term policy favouring rail over road. As the motorway network spread, transport cafés declined. The Ace got seedier, drugs were dealt there, and Alan Hendry commented, "I don't like my girls nearly as hard as some of these [regulars] had become," with the empty train carriages on the sidings above the arches experiencing frequent couplings of the non-railway kind. The café closed in 1969.

By then, thanks to rising wages and to cheap cars exemplified by the classless Mini, not only had car traffic increased from one car per 6.1 households in 1951 to one per 1.5 households in 1969, but many young people were beginning their driving lives on four wheels, not two. Early in 1967 a blanket 70mph upper speed limit had been imposed. British motorcycles didn't disappear – there were glory days in production racing where supremacy swung from BSA to Triumph, was contested by Royal Enfield, taken decisively by Norton and then regained by Triumph. But the bulk of the product, after the home market

The author interviews Mark Wilsmore upstairs at the Ace during the early days of the café's revival.

Triumph ruled. Crowds stunned by the '65 Thruxton T120 Bonneville. A unit 650 twin, "but there were plenty still ready to sell their soul for it on the never-never."

slumped from 1960 on – for 1961 UK sales were down by 35% on the previous year – was aimed, very successfully for a time, at export, mostly to America.

From 1963 the market leaders BSA/Triumph, for reasons of economy and ease of expanded production, switched their big bike motors, which were still of the same twin-cylinder design, to unitary construction of the engine and gearbox. As Mike Clay wrote, the BSA unit twins "to the café crowd were hideous…on a big 650 [the 'power-egg' style] looks wrong…a big bike engine needs to look knobbly." As for the unit Triumphs, "The 650s lost much of their charisma… Café racers everywhere hated it." As the late Triumph rebuild guru and ex-Meriden tester Hughie Hancox put it, the unit engine also lost a lot of give, and forgiveness, offering a generally harsher (if better-handling) ride than the pre-units. Which, with their longer cases, were also for many the only engines to use for building a well-proportioned Triton.

Even more than these particulars, the Zeitgeist, the spirit of the age, moved on from the Rockers, who went from an archetype, affectionately recognised in

lovingly detailed cartoons by Giles of the *Daily Express*, to a disgruntled minority. From 1963, new blues-based music, the increasing use of marijuana, and girls with long hair, short skirts, and love lives liberated by the Pill, saw youth dance off in another direction, with the media spotlight close behind. Folk-rock declared war on war itself, specifically in Vietnam. A page turned, the river flowed.

But still, as Bob Innes put it, "A lot of people, their life stopped when the Ace closed." Mark Wilsmore, the man who would successfully re-open the Ace in 2001, stated that "Every rider of that generation remembers the place and it's a treasured memory, even if they only came once, or never came at all." The recognition of that ephemeral moment when some young outsiders took it to the limit, and in doing so created an instantly recognisable style, is confirmed by tribute groups from Nashville to Nagasaki. The machines you will read about, products of an industry that would self-destruct just a dozen years after most of them had been built, were the unlikely expression of a spirit which has not died.

CHAPTER 2:
VINCENT SERIES C BLACK SHADOW

"Legendary" is not too strong a word for Vincent's post-war vee-twin. It was a superlative, different in every way, beginning with its place of manufacture – a small factory at Stevenage in Hertfordshire employing just 400, well away from the Midlands manufacturing heartland. Essentially it was the fruit of a collaboration between two talented individuals, Philip Vincent (PCV) the firm's founder, and the Australian design engineer Phil Irving. It was the only British vee-twin roadster produced post-war until the Hesketh came along in 1982, the only British 1000cc motorcycle then apart from the Ariel Square Four, and at the top end, 1948's Series C in a straight line would be the fastest production two-wheeled machine for the next 20 years.

In those pre-motorway days, *The Motor Cycle* could find nowhere to achieve the maximum speed with a Black Shadow, while *Motor Cycling* recorded a maximum of 122mph, with 87 in second and 110 in third. Vincents, at a time when many motorcycles retained a rigid rear end, featured a sophisticated cantilever twinned or monoshock system of rear suspension, dreamed up by PCV in the 1920s and stubbornly adhered to by him until production of his motorcycles ended in 1955, coincidentally roughly the start of the Rocker era.

DREAM MACHINE

Philip Vincent had bought the racer Howard Davies' defunct HRD company, TT winners in the 1920s, its machines classically finished in deep, gold-lined black; so until 1949 the marque was known as Vincent-HRD. Phil Irving arrived from Oz in the UK in 1930 as passenger on a Vincent-framed sidecar outfit, and after a spell at Velocette, became Vincent's unofficial chief designer in 1932. The majority of the Vincent's essential features were determined by the two men's work together. They became friends, and the older, experienced Australian balanced PCV's buoyant, creative nature.

This is the Early Series B Black Shadow used for both Motor Cycling *and* The Motor Cycle *road tests in Spring 1948. The latter involved a 2400-mile trip over the Alps to Italy. Note earlier, lighter Brampton forks.*

Series C Black Shadow: the ultimate timeless classic?

From sprung saddle to cantilevered rear suspension and Girdraulic front forks, the Vincent was its own man.

After using proprietary engines, Irving in three months designed their own 500 single for 1935; like Velocette's M-Series, it featured high camshafts, but the Vincent's layout had a novel valve and valve gear arrangement, with splayed pushrods, transverse rockers, and unique double valve guides. Asked why it featured a relatively short 84mm stroke in contrast to the longer one on Norton singles, Irving claimed it was "because that was big enough for me to get a hand down to clean it"! The cylinder design, which would be retained on the twins, ensured cool running and high mileages between de-cokes.

The birth of the big twin had a fated quality, as one day in 1936 Irving casually superimposed two tracings

of the single engine's timing side – or were they disturbed into that position by a breeze? – to come up with a vee-twin that could be created with minimum new tooling. The result, again achieved in three months, was the Series A Rapide, "the Snarling Beast" or alternatively "the plumber's nightmare", the latter epithet because of the external oil pump and four external oil-lines. It offered 108mph performance, the effortless power PCV desired, and with the spring frame, unprecedentedly agile handling for a big vee. But the power could overwhelm the bought-in Burman gearbox and clutch, and for a luxury roadster competing with the Brough Superior, it lacked the latter's unified styling. Just 78 were built by the tiny operation before war came.

During the war, Irving became formally Vincent's Chief Engineer, and he and PCV formulated the A's successor. The latter's long 58-inch wheelbase would be shortened 2 inches by their own massive gearbox internals being built in unit with the engine, along with their own design of servo clutch to counter the previous problems. These would be housed in deep crankcases, cast, like the cylinder barrels and heads, in alloy. As Phil Irving put it, while steel post-war was in short supply with quotas limited to export-friendly

1949 Series C Black Shadow with Girdraulic forks. Vincents remained badged H.R.D. until late in 1949.

"A thicket of timing gears." These are race-prepared engines with the gears drilled for lightness.

Black is Beautiful. And this Shadow was recently timed at a certified 122mph at Bruntingthorpe.

Ride the Snarling Beast and you'd best keep your eye on the ball.

industries, "There was plenty of aluminium available from melting down crashed or obsolete aircraft … to [dissipate heat], reduce weight and avoid chrome plating … aluminium in various alloys was used extensively". PCV always sought to eliminate the possibility of rust on his creations —–the works included a rust-proofing plant – so items like brake rods, the pivot on the hinged rear mudguard, banjo unions, and the Tommy bars found on the axles, components which on motorcycles would usually be chrome plated, for Vincents were in stainless steel. The alloy castings were done by Mason and Burns of Walsall, so there was a connection with the Midlands heartland after all.

The massive and very rigid 240lb engine/gearbox, with its internally-webbed crankcase, became part of the structural whole, standing in for a conventional frame's front downtube and cradle. The engine was suspended from a substantial 16-gauge short box-type triangular structure. Stung by the "Plumber's Nightmare" jibes, the new engine was relatively uncluttered externally, because this upper frame beam doubled up as the 6-pint oil tank, with the filler cap incorporated into the petrol tank beside the petrol cap, and the oilways now all internal drillings, bar the pipes to and from the internal oil pump. Behind the beam lay Vincent's own slanted twin spring boxes, plus later, on the Series C, a hydraulic unit, for the rear suspension. At the front, since PCV abominated telescopic forks with their variation in wheelbase and their dive under braking, light but strong proprietary Brampton girder forks were bought in, further distinguishing the Vincent in the telescopic age.

The result, the Series B, was offered in standard 45bhp Rapide form for 1947, with the 55bhp sports Black Shadow following for 1948. The Shadow featured a slightly higher compression, though still only 7.3:1 in view of the low octane Pool petrol then solely available; a higher bottom gear; bigger bore (1⅛in) twin remote float Amal carburettors mounted one on each side of the engine; and polished internals, including the con rods. But the crucial difference in performance seems to have come from the selective assembly of the engine components. On the cycle parts, the brakes, back-to-back 7-inch "duo" anchors front and rear with potentially formidable stopping power – 22ft from 30mph was recorded on one test, when most machines struggled to achieve 30ft – on the Shadow featured cooling ribs, far from ornamental in the heat of fast riding.

The other thing you paid for was the spectacular though understated appearance of power, as the whole engine was finished in baked-on heat-dispersant deep black paint. PCV was as particular about finish as you would expect, with his own stove-enamelling plant at Stevenage. Before the alloy parts were stoved black, the "Pylumin" treatment was applied, to provide a surface key for the finest Pinchin and Johnson rubber undercoat and black enamel paint to stick to. They were then hand-lined in gold leaf. The black engine, breathing muscular power, set off the short, splayed stainless steel pushrod tubes, topped by the bulging knuckles of big domed hexagonal rocker-cap nuts. These, and the large, neat single timing cover, were embossed with the H.R.D. initials until 1949, when American distributors had pointed out that the latter were too easily mistaken for the home-grown H.D., Harley-Davidson. After that, ones with "Vincent" were phased in. The Shadow's crowning glory was the very large and prominent Smiths 5-inch speedometer,

The separate float chamber on a long arm for the rear Amal 289 carburettor which fed the inlet port on the right of the cylinder. The Shadow's carb, unlike the Rapide's, featured a cross-stud that braced the ears at the rear corner of the petrol tank.

Towers of power, topped by bunched metal knuckles. The Shadow engine's dramatic all-black finish was also heat-dispersant.

The front cylinder's carburettor was on the left, and most were brass-bodied. Note the rear cylinder's pronounced off-set to the left, countering the vee-twin problem of overheating back pots.

mounted proudly near-vertical, forward of the black-painted handlebars, and calibrated to 150mph.

Both Irving and PCV were active motorcyclists (until a 1947 crash testing a Rapide which put Philip Vincent off work for months and curtailed his riding), and part of their design philosophy was to include where possible well thought out touches which would make life easier for a rider, anywhere in the world. In the event of a puncture, while for other manufacturers a QD (quickly detachable) rear wheel was often an extra if it was offered at all, and still involved the use of tools, on Vincents the rear wheel could be removed in 35 seconds, with no tools, by releasing the torque arms for the brakes via their spring clips; unfastening, with the built-in stainless steel Tommy bar, the rear spindle; then pushing the wheel forward, hooking the chain off the sprocket, and extracting the wheel rear-ward thanks to the hinged rear mudguard section with its substantial pivot pin, again in stainless. The front wheel too featured a spindle with Tommy bar. To aid work on the engine without having to remove it, the entire front end, or the frame beam, or the whole rear fork, could be quickly removed, with the two prop stands, one on each side to suit the roads of home or export markets, able to combine to form a centre stand supporting what was left at the front, or the rear stand be used at the back. The kickstart could also be fitted to the right or to the left, to suit right-hand sidecar outfits.

Dual 6-inch front brakes, set up properly, were highly effective. Shadow's drums were made differently for front and rear wheels.

The shaped Feridax dualseat had been adopted from the first, half a dozen years before other manufacturers realised that this, rather than sprung saddles, was what riders and passengers wanted. On the Series C, the seat was attached to the cantilever unit, meaning that the rear of the seat rose and fell with the back wheel, producing an unusual sensation, bouncy over rough surfaces – but infinitely preferable to the jarring shocks transmitted by a rigid rear end, or by the crude plunger springing often in general use till after 1954. The Black Shadow's alloy mudguards neatly hugged the contours of the big wheels (20 x 3.0 inch front, 19 x 3.50 inch rear), and started a fashion for similar aftermarket items for café racers.

The 3½-gallon petrol tank's gentle curve from front to back was both aesthetically pleasing and deliberately designed so that inside the tank any debris could accumulate at the rear, in the small recess below the

Girdraulic forks, which replaced the previous, lighter Bramptons, were massively strong and featured a heavier (180lb) spring.

level of the twin petrol taps. The graceful sweep of the twin exhausts saw them both exiting from the front of their respective cylinders for optimum cooling, then siamesing and running back to a single long silencer. All the controls were highly adjustable, the foot levers being drilled for that purpose. Control cables had double-wound outer casings. The wheel spokes reversed normal practice and were laced into the hub, thus relieving tension on the brake drums.

The Black Shadow reached what most consider its peak (though like everything about Vincents, this can be disputed) with the Series C for 1949, though these machines would overlap with the B. The C's principal distinguishing feature was the new Girdraulic fork at its front end (though some early Cs went out with Bramptons, due to the Bristol Aircraft Company getting behind with component deliveries). The Girdraulics were designed to combine the qualities, like a constant wheelbase, of girder forks, and the softer, hydraulically damped action of telescopics. They featured fork blades of aluminium alloy, from the Bristol Aircraft Company, and one-piece links, the

Trademark 5-inch 150mph speedo. And even the handlebars were black. The second filler cap was for the oil compartment.

Finned brakes distinguished Shadow from Rapide. Note built-in stainless steel Tommy bar, enabling rear wheel removal without tools.

Series C featured damper unit between slanted spring boxes.

upper ones in heat-treated alloy, the others steel forgings. The links moved on ground-steel spindles in Oilite bushes. Long, enclosed barrel springs behind the blades could be repositioned on eccentric mountings at their top end, to vary strength and trail. Irving was "a rabid [sidecar] chairman" himself, and eccentrics in the bottom fork link were incorporated with the upper ends of the fork springs attached to it, so that when new, the fork springs could be instantly adjusted for solo or sidecar use. A Vincent-made unit mounted forward of the steering head provided the hydraulic damping. Girdraulics were longer and heavier than Bramptons – some riders, including George Brown, the works record-breaking sprinter and racer, preferred the latter – with immense torsional rigidity and strength (one owner hit a Triumph Herald car which was written off, but

though his front wheel was buckled in two, the fork's adjustment remained within a thou. of standard).

Other distinguishing features of the C were that the lug for the seat stays was curved, where the B's had been straight. And the C also mounted a two-way hydraulic damper between the slanted pair of Vincent's own suspension units under the seat.

Meanwhile there was a string of business troubles at the little company, and an Official Receiver was called in for 1950. But he proved sympathetic, and the firm's fortunes revived, with maximum production achieved in 1952, so that the majority of Vincent's post-war motorcycles were Series C twins. Even so, the entire post-war total was only to be around 11,000 machines, between a half and a third of a good single year's production at Triumph. And the penalty for increased production was some corner-cutting,

The World's Fastest Standard Motorcycle

combined with jigs and fixtures becoming worn, and over time a shortage of specialists as the best men moved on: a case in point was Phil Irving, who returned to Australia in 1949, after which development faltered. All this meant that some felt the quality on later bikes could be uneven compared to earlier ones. But Norman Peach, a wheel-builder and test rider at Stevenage for the whole period, offered a different perspective. "Most post-war equipment was rather worn out. It wasn't until the early Fifties, when production increased, that they got some more up-to-date stuff. Till then, it did hold things up." Norman, however, was another who preferred Brampton forks to Girdraulics.

Nevertheless, the mighty Vincent's reputation kept growing – as the publicity emphasised, the Black Shadow was "The World's Fastest Standard Motorcycle – this is a fact NOT a slogan". Though at 1000cc it was excluded from most top-level racing, which was limited to 500cc or under, the Black Shadow and its racing derivative the Black Lightning, only about 30 of which were built, achieved sensational results in hill-climbing and sprinting (George Brown's "Gunga Din" had started life as a Rapide rejected by the test department), and in the short-lived 1000cc Clubmans TT which Stevenage twins won three times. In 1948 in America, a wealthy journalist fancied owning and riding around on the fastest motorcycle in the country. So Vincent prepared a special for him, and at Bonneville salt flats his rider, Rollie Free, did a 148mph run, then stripped to just a bathing suit and shoes, lay horizontal with his mid-section on the rear mudguard and, changing gear by hand, hoisted his speed to 156mph, an AMA Class A record. The machine was then returned to street legal trim, and the journalist had his wish. In 1955 in New Zealand, Russell Wright on a streamlined Black Lightning raised the world solo motorcycle record to 185mph on a wet road outside Christchurch, and with Bob Burns the next day took the world sidecar record at 162mph.

There was also fun to be had with the Vin's effortless superiority, particularly in America where street-racing for money against the home-grown Harley vee-twin opposition involved reaching flat-out neck-and-neck speed, at which point the Vincenteer would simply change into top and walk away. There were also incidents like the touring Vincent rider with his wife on the pillion who came upon a hill-climb where none of the local men had been able to reach the top. He rode up it successfully, and down again; then his wife repeated the performance before the couple proceeded on their way. Back in Blighty Alan Jackson, founder of the Vincent Owners Club (VOC), was approached about joining the Pall Mall

Club, which apparently involved riding your Vincent through Admiralty Arch at the legal limit, then accelerating to 100mph before you reached the Buckingham Palace roundabout…

This was a suitably upmarket venue for a machine which was exclusive by its nature – 135,000-mile Vincent man and VMCC founder "Titch""Allen stated that the twin "demanded a rider of rare judgment to exploit its potential" – as well as by its limited production numbers, even more so in the UK as some 80% were exported; and, definitively, by its price. In late 1949, a Triumph 6T 650 Thunderbird cost £194, a Morris Minor car £338, and a Vincent Black Shadow £425. The gap would narrow a little, with a 1954 Triumph 650 Tiger 110 costing £240 when a '54 Black Shadow was down to £348, but that was still well over half a year's wages for a skilled man.

The Black Shadow's character was summed up by World Champion racer John Surtees, who as a young

In a striking variation of colour scheme, just over 20 of these Chinese Red Series C Shadows were produced for the American market.

A 1954 Black Lightning racer.

Black Lightning racer supplied by Humphreys of London. Every one was different.

Vincent star sprinter/racer George Brown ended up adapting his own competition machines to swinging-arm suspension and telescopic front forks.

man had undertaken an engineering apprenticeship at Stevenage and raced a Grey Flash single impressively, as well as converting and riding his father's Black Lightning. "The joy of the Vincent is that you don't have to rev it. There is an enormous amount of torque, so although you can take it to 7000 [rpm] you are normally better off changing gear at 6." He went on to say that the engine picked up easily and delivered power lazily, not fussily. Vincent adverts also emphasised that the Black Shadow was "a tractable sports model not a super sports or racing machine," and as PCV had originally envisioned, "a design of the perfect luxury, high speed, long distance touring

motorcycle," which would "eliminate distance with contemptuous ease."

With a tall top gear meaning that 100mph came up at half throttle and 4500rpm, the big vee-twins were tireless all-day cruisers, as fast and stable two-up with luggage as they were solo, and as another of their slogans proudly put it, "built up to a standard, not down to a price." If well fettled they were stable at any speed, and their road-holding was such that the early design of circular clutch cover had to be replaced by one with a cutaway at the bottom after the first ones had been worn away by enthusiastic cornering on left-handers. VOC members recorded extremely high mileages on their machines, such as 350,000, without major attention.

The Black Shadow continued little changed until 1955, which saw the new Series D, the only development of the twins which Vincent undertook without Irving. The Ds are mostly remembered for the visually striking faired versions, the Black Prince (Shadow) and Black Knight (Rapide), with their all-over fibreglass panelling. PCV had anticipated by decades the cover-up in plastic of modern sports motorcycles, leapfrogging the partial metal panelling offered by Triumph a couple of years later. But reactions were mixed and even apathetic to the new range, even though unfaired versions continued to be offered as well. The D featured coil ignition and revised suspension, with the twin shocks replaced by a single, softer-sprung unit from Armstrong, plus a higher, plain rear seat and subframe. But motorcycling was in a slump, production could only continue if prices were raised, and though the order book was apparently full, late that year PCV decided to end production. As the veteran

journalist Ixion put it, "Quivers of real grief shook the entire Commonwealth."

IN THE BELLY OF THE BEAST

At the heart of it all had lain that mighty motor. The Vincent twin engine, to start at the bottom, featured deep crankcases of DTD 24 aircraft-specification alloy, vertically split in the British way and with massive internal ribbing, providing the strength needed for the engine to play its part as a stressed frame member. The thick-walled cases also damped down vibration to help achieve the twins' legendary smooth running.

The crankshaft inside the cases was a large built-up one, with nickel chrome steel mainshafts pressed into the forged flywheels, which were of 40 ton carbon steel, machined all over and jig-drilled for balance. After pressing in, one raised face flange, together with the outside diameter of each, were ground off the mainshaft centres, to make the flywheels exactly true to the shafts. The ground locations were subsequently used to position the flywheels for the boring and facing of the crankpin holes, guaranteeing a high degree of accuracy for the flywheel assembly's true running, and again for the engine's smoothness.

The crankshaft ran on two pairs of main bearings, a roller plus a ball race on the drive side and twinned roller races on the timing side, a very long-lasting set-up. The mainshafts were splined on the drive side to take the narrow, three-lobe engine shaft shock absorber, with its 18 pairs of small springs; Phil Irving later revealed that this design had stemmed from post-war production constraints, as the necessary heavy steel wire for a conventional single spring had been in short supply. The little springs could be fragile.

The alloy cylinder barrels were mounted at a nominal 50 degrees to suit available magnetos (the C Black Shadow used a Lucas KVF) – "nominal", since the excellent VOC spares scheme discovered "everything between a 48 degree and a 52 degree angle," presumably due to machining variations. As Vincent road tester Norman Peach put it: "So many people today think that Vincents were made to jewellery spec. This wasn't true – they were financially constrained production things."

The rear cylinder was offset 1¼ inches to the left, to help supply cooling air for it and avoid the known vee-twin problem of overheating back pots. High grade cast iron liners were centrifugally shrunk into the alloy cylinders, and for more rigidity, the extensions below the jackets were deeply spigotted into the massive upper throat of the crankcase.

The connecting rods were of forged nickel chrome steel, running side-by-side on the same 1⅞-inch diameter crankpin of EN36 case-hardened mild chrome steel. The big ends, unusually, featured uncaged roller bearings, but these proved perfectly durable for the relatively low-revving roadsters. Pistons were of aluminium, the Black Shadow's giving 7.3:1 compression against the Rapide's 6.8:1.

On the timing side, behind the cover, lay what one owner described as "a forest of timing gears," with a large, intermediate gear wheel, initially of phosphor bronze, meshing with each camshaft gear; there were separate high-mounted camshafts for each cylinder. The teeth of the timing gears were fine-pitch and the idler gear spindle was adjustable, so that tooth backlash could be dialled out. The two camshafts were carried on fixed spindles, supported by aluminium steady plates to help keep them parallel however hot the engine became.

The front camshaft gear also drove a timed breather idler, and this meshed with the forward-mounted magneto, which featured platinum points to assist starting. The magneto sat ahead of the crankcase under a protective alloy shield, whose distinctive zig-zag edge could be seen from the drive side. The electrics other than ignition relied upon a Miller chain-driven 50-watt dynamo, positioned behind the rear cylinder. Oil often penetrated this, and over time disabled it.

The camshafts were operated by flat-faced lever-type cam followers with their pivots located below the camshafts, not above them, to do away with the pre-war A's separate cam covers. The camshafts operated the short, wide-splayed 6-inch pushrods in their stainless steel tunnels, the latter sometimes a source of oil leaks. High-mounted camshafts eliminated flexing and hence valve bounce, while maintaining accurate valve timing. The pushrods had been positioned to

Swansong. Fully enclosed 1955 Black Prince twin.

match the angle of the valves, which was unusual because the rockers lay across the engine. Both valve gear and cylinder heads were of heat-treated RR 53B aircraft-spec aluminium alloy, with the heads' combustion chambers hemispherical, carrying the 1.8-inch diameter sili-chrome steel inlet valve and the 1.67-inch diameter DTD 49B steel exhaust valve. The latter, running hotter, had a valve seat of aluminium bronze, while the inlet seat was of austenitic iron, whose work-hardening properties resisted seal wear.

Derived from Irving's 1934 design for the single, the rockers unusually operated against a hardened contact collar located midway down the stem between the upper and lower valve guides, with the springs above the collar isolated from engine heat. These unique double valve guides were employed to ensure that wear was low. Enclosed coil valve springs helped keep the cylinders' height down. Separate caps gave access to the valves, while the big embossed hexagonal ones unscrewed to reach the forged steel rockers and their adjusters. The rockers were mounted on unorthodox "cotton reel" pivot blocks clamped into the cylinder head castings' integral rocker chambers. The front and rear cylinder heads differed from each other, to optimize the angle of the front carburettor, and this front head was the one easiest for tuners to open up without breaking through into the rocker tunnel, as could happen at the rear; so front heads can sometimes be found on the rear cylinder too – just one of many, many ways in which Vincent owners modified and individualised their machines. Both heads featured well-finned, forward-facing exhaust ports for optimum cooling. Both were held down by 65 ton bolts into massive anchorages in the crankcase, the ultra-strong bolts also being part of the engine-mounting system.

Lubrication was via a Pilgrim duplex rotary plunger pump, operated by a worm drive off the timing side of the camshaft. The precision-made pump was housed in an accurately bored cylinder formed in the lower part of the timing case. Chosen to avoid the problem for owners of wet-sumping, often found with gear-type pumps, in practice the pump's delivery was meagre, and not helped by the tortuous internal oil passages – but this was never to represent a problem. The pump feed passed through an integral cylindrical oil filter cast at the front of the timing side crankcase. The only two external oil lines were the feed and return pipes to the "beam" tank, with the return pipe, to lubricate the valve guide, coupled to the rocker bearing housing via a banjo and banjo bolt.

A drawing office error (nobody's perfect) meant that when the engine was running, the top of the lower exhaust valve guide was barely above the level of circulating oil in the rocker box. At low revs in town running, oil thus ran down the guides and fouled the spark plugs, especially on the front cylinder where the inlet tunnel was near horizontal, and thus failed to drain as well as that of the rear one. Early on, grooves were cut in the underside of the rocker bearings to assist drainage, but problems persisted.

The twins' transmission had been designed robustly enough to take future power hikes, with primary drive by triplex ⅜in pitch chain, with a leaf-spring tensioner easily adjusted by a screw under the case. Gearing options existed, including a reversible rear sprocket to provide either solo or sidecar ratios. The gearbox, built in unit, featured crossover operation, so that alone of all the motorcycles we shall consider here, the Vincent's rear drive chain was on the right. All gears were of case-hardened EN 36 nickel chrome steel and the compact design's internals, though dictating deliberate changes, were near-indestructible. The gearchange like the other controls was adjustable, but the early linkage system had been over-complicated, further contributing to heavy changes. A new pedal was adopted for 1952, the same year that the Black Shadow adopted the Rapide's lower first gear.

The Series A had proved that conventional clutches were pressed to cope with the twins' power output. PCV designed something highly original which in fact comprised two clutches. A single-plate primary clutch with light springs was located in an allegedly oil-tight circular housing set in the primary chaincase cover. This provided the pressure to expand a pair of shoes, like drum brake shoes, in a ribbed drum. This self-servo arrangement began to operate at around 50mph, and bit harder and harder as speeds rose.

The design caused two problems. Moving off from a standstill was always unpredictable, as the exact point when the clutch bit was variable, and could even be affected by the weather. This could be irritating, but more serious was that despite several oil seals, and a later change for the shoes' lining to material claimed to be impervious to oil, in fact lubricant would find its way along the splines of the mainshaft and onto the shoes, causing bad clutch slip. The simplest though partial solution was to drill holes in the bottom of the housing to let the oil out. A further negative point was that the servo-clutch's weight contributed to the heavy, necessarily deliberate gearchange.

THE KING AND THE CAFÉ CROWD

This superbly robust and tireless engine/gearbox unit would clearly propel a Vincent farther and faster, to the off-beat rhythm of its glorious exhaust note, than any standard production motorcycle in its time and

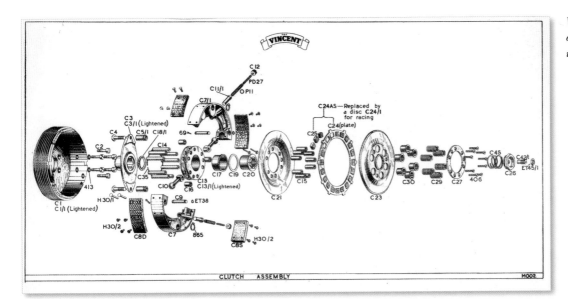

Vincent two-stage clutch. An original idea, but it proved vulnerable to oil.

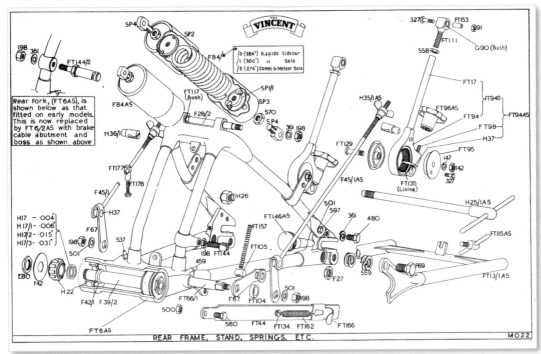

Vincent Series C rear suspension.

for many years to come, untroubled at high speed by the vibration inherent in any parallel twin design. So why did the café racer crowd not embrace it more enthusiastically? Scarcity and price had always been factors. With production at Stevenage ceasing after 1955, certainly Vincents, singles as well as twins, had featured in "the flying jacket time" of the mid-Fifties, but relatively few thereafter, when the Rockers subsisted on a diet of parallel twins with the occasional fast single, despite secondhand prices for Vincents being risibly low by today's standards.

One clue stems from the fact that there had been trouble in Paradise even while Vincents were still being made. Their top sprinter and racer, the forth-right George Brown, had spelt it out as he saw it: "I was the chief tester of an obsolete machine which could have been so very much better. We had superb engines crying out for a modern frame." But PCV remained convinced of his original triangulated, cantilever arrangement. Brown favoured a conventional swinging-arm on his legendary sprinter Nero, after he had left the company in 1952. History in the form of today's monoshocks has vindicated PCV, but at the time, the construction of the spring boxes and of the hydraulic units front and rear was not the equal of modern replacements, and the same went for the

Factory tester and VOC (Vincent Owners Club) mainstay Ted Davies on his personal Shadow, with non-standard headlamp, in the snow. Vincent pilots were a hardy breed.

struts in the Girdraulic fork.

The young John Surtees had found that though his Girdraulic-forked Grey Flash "could be laid over, [it] was not the finest for dealing with rippled surfaces. There is quite a lot of friction in a link-type fork," and he went on to detail another little-known drawing office design fault in the forks, which had only been discovered too late, after the expensive tooling had been made: too much anti-dive action had been built in, and the angles of the links had, crucially, to be correctly set in order to reduce this. The front fork spindles had to have no end float, yet had to be totally free, or the rider did not know quite where the front wheel was, and whether it was bouncing over or absorbing small bumps. Even set up perfectly, said Surtees, despite the admirable absence of dive, it suffered from the lack of available movement, so that both wheels skipped slightly when the brakes were applied.

Surtees, like Brown, would modify his father's Black Lightning, and then in 1954, slot it into a Manx Norton Featherbed frame, creating what he thought might have been the first ever Norvin. (The latter hybrid never felt desirable to me, mainly due to weight distribution issues. Café racer and special builder Mike Clay's reservation was just weight, with both the heavy engine and the weight of the conven-

tional frame.)

In the cafés it was often a case of qualified admiration for Vincent twins. Tony Hazelwood, an active rider up to 1956, told Duckworth that in the early Fifties "fast standard machines were either too expensive or just not available" – the big vees ticked both boxes – and went on, "Vincents were King but the handling was not great." Tom Thackeray called a Black Shadow "a nice bike but it needed a lot of tinkering, especially to keep both carbs in synch." Vincent B and C carburettors were handed, and if the wrong one was fitted to the wrong side, the holes in the jet-block body which contained the pilot jet might not line up. On some twins the front and rear carb required different jets, with the rear ones, counter-intuitively, needing the bigger jets. And the Black Shadow's front one was unique in being sand-cast in brass.

The Rocker urge to tweak and improve was inappropriate when applied to Vincents; an American distributor stated, "The only problems I had were guys who wouldn't leave them alone – the carbs were a little touchy to get synchronized. The people that left them alone and did nothing but ride them had no problems." But that was not the Rocker hands-on way. And bodgers did not need to apply. As factory man Norman Peach put it, "Many Vincent owners were mechanically capable enough to strip their own engines…To my mind…if you own a Vincent, you've got to have a reasonable amount of mechanical expertise."

By the '58 -'62 ton-up heyday, Series Cs, though massively durable, could be getting on for ten years old, and very likely would have been ridden hard, far and fast. From that era the late Peter Brown, then a ton-up lad from Wigan way, recalled that "The Vincent Rapide…went like stink in a straight line but God help you on corners or if you wanted to come to an abrupt halt." The duo brakes, so excellent when new and correctly set up, could be difficult to adjust if you didn't know what you were doing – the "far" side needed adjusting first – and were never great in the wet.

The handling is something every Vincent owner has an opinion about, but for the cut and thrust of street racing it was probably not ideal, and lesser breeds could make up time against a Vincent twin on the bends. Racer Ken Bills wrote (of the singles, but they shared their chassis and fork design with the twins) that they "didn't fall naturally into corners, they seemed heavy and needed conscious effort to change course, and you couldn't go through the swervery so quickly." And of course the twins were heavy at 458lbs, nearly 65lbs heavier than a Triumph T110; no other British twin would be that heavy until the last, 466lb Norton Commando 850 Mk 3 in 1975. Factory man Norman Peach also observed that "the Series C with Girdraulics was taller at the front, which to my mind made handling less positive."

The Beast's handling undoubtedly could be, and was, learned by many, and the twin remained undisputed guv'nor over distance, but for the café-to-café dash there were other disadvantages. Kickstarting 998cc of vee-twin, despite the magneto's platinum points, could be tricky. Norman Peach again: "There's a technique, of course…too many people stop three-quarters of the way down their kick – you have to give it a little flick at the end, to get the flywheels going." The slipping clutch was a frequent unwelcome feature. The heavy, slow gearchange lost out to potentially slick changes from Norton and Triumph boxes. The Vincent's oil took an unusually long dozen miles to warm up, more than the distance from the Ace to the Bee, and if the motor was thrashed before that, rapid wear could ensue.

Ray Knight, a fast Johnson's cowboy in the late Fifties who would go on to win the 500 Production TT in 1968 on a T100 Triumph Daytona, discovered with his Black Shadow that "Vincent twins didn't like being subjected to the same sort of revolutions as the vertical twins of the day." He could "only just see off a local acquaintance who reckoned he was the local top

man on his Triumph 650 T110." Ray's Shadow could only just top 110mph, and ridden thus, suffered "a couple of blown gearboxes, and camshafts that lost their humps, [with] cam spindles that came loose in the timing case later." (Camshafts were one element of the engine for which the company had had to outsource production, with sometimes variable quality resulting.) After a period on 600cc Norton 99 and BSA A10 650 twins, he got another Black Shadow cheap because it was rattling, which he correctly diagnosed as broken shock absorber springs, "having had to renew several sets on my earlier model." But still the Black Shadow's vaunted top speeds in the 120s remained elusive. "On a two mile downhill straight, hiding behind the 5 inch 150 mph speedo dial, I would try to urge the needle…just a fraction further…Flat out, the Shadow would clock no more than 112 mph, and I must have tried 20 or 30 times." Ray moved on.

Expensive spares and repairs didn't sit well with lads operating on a shoestring, and mpg at around 47 looked poor beside a 650 Triumph's figure of around 65. The Black Shadow's "restrained and sober appearance" as an advert put it, while undoubtedly classic, was not quite rock'n'roll. Though its superiority was ungrudgingly accepted, as journalist and editor Cyril Ayton, who owned one in the Sixties, hesitantly suggested, "These bikes commanded respect for technical excellence while failing to inspire affection that some demonstrably inferior bikes – like, for example, a Triumph twin – could so easily manage."

However, let's not forget the thundering roar of a Vincent 1000 on full song, and the way the horizon rushed towards you and "suddenly there were bends where before on other machines the road had been straight".

TECHNICAL SPECIFICATIONS:
1949 VINCENT SERIES C BLACK SHADOW

Capacity	998cc
Bore	84mm
Stroke	90mm
Compression	7.3:1
Power output	55bhp @ 5700rpm
Electrical system	6 volt
Ignition	Lucas KVF magneto
Generator	Miller 50 watt dynamo
Wheels and Tyres	F: 3.00 x 21, R: 3.50 x 19 in
Brakes	F and R: twinned 7 x 7/8-inch drums
Weight	458lbs
Mean Maximum Speeds	1st: 68mph, 2nd: 87mph, 3rd: 110mph, 4th: Not obtained

CHAPTER 3:
SINGLES:
BSA GOLD STAR DBD 34
AND VELOCETTE VENOM

Clubmans Gold Star

BSA GOLD STAR

After the Vincent twins, by 1957 BSA's competition-bred Gold Star singles were some of the fastest, toughest, most charismatic and best-handling machines you could buy. But as with the Vincent, response from the Rockers, while admiring, was qualified. In 1960, a Busy Bee regular named Charlie Williams told Duckworth, "Goldies were the fastest things around at the time…", but others found that for café racing they took too long to get up to speed. The Ace's prominent black rider and regular, Cecil Richards, did try a Gold Star,

but after a puncture-induced bad crash, reverted to an A10 Super Rocket.

It was no secret that a Clubmans Goldie with its 9.0:1 or higher compression and 1½-inch GP carb could be very difficult to start, especially hot. The leading specialist at the time, Capt. Eddie Dow in Banbury, who had won the 1955 Senior Clubmans TT on one, more recently conceded that under normal roadgoing conditions "the Gold Star owner couldn't cope with the 'cammy' motor" (power only came in at around 3500rpm due to the large

amount of valve overlap), "and the Goldie was expensive to maintain."

Also, being built in limited numbers, they were not always easy to find and buy. The close-ratio gearboxes necessary for best performance meant clutch-slipping up to at least 30mph to get away cleanly, a procedure which, if it had to be repeated too often in traffic, quickly used up the not-too-impressive BSA 6-spring clutch. Another performance necessity, the semi-megaphone sports "twittering" silencer, was anti-socially noisy in the extreme. And in general, big single-cylinder motorcycles had begun to be yesterday's men with the 1937 advent of Triumph's Speed Twin, and by the mid-Fifties were perceived as such by many younger riders.

But the Goldie was one exception, almost unique in being painstakingly developed for on- and off-road competition – genuinely race-bred, yet £100 cheaper than exotic ohc track racers, and since it resembled its B31/B33 cooking cousins, much easier to work on. And it did have a following. Dow's mechanic John Gleed recalled that when the Banbury shop opened around 1958, "It was just the right time…People rode

in from everywhere, on a Saturday morning it was like the Isle of Man TT pits out in the lane. There was a craze for fitting our fibreglass petrol tanks, and people would buy them from us and dump their old steel tanks by the road. At the end of Saturday afternoon there'd be tanks, exhausts, standard seats, littered all

DBD34 was a bike that looked as good from the drive side, where the swell of the cylinder could be fully relished, as it did from the timing side.

Competition bred: Gold Star-mounted Arthur Lampkin contesting the Lancs Grand National scramble.

Gold Star CB Clubmans of 1954.

over the pavement – incredible!"

The final DBD34 500 in particular possessed a unique, muscular appeal. You could cruise one comfortably at 65mph in top, but that same speed was obtainable in the famously tall first gear, and as latter day specialist Phil Pearson put it, "With a Gold Star, there's no enjoyment riding it slow. If you're going to have a Gold Star, you're going to have to ride." Which would have suited the ton-up boys. But many found a run-and-bump start was easier than kickstarting. An easy-starting Triumph twin could be in the next county by the time you'd managed that.

Both the engines and cycle parts were strong and quick – a 1955 DB Clubmans 500 was tested by *Motor Cycling* at over 110mph. The year before, prior

Clubmans in action: racer Eddie Crooks gets down to it in 1956.

to BSA successfully contesting the Daytona Beach races in Florida, development engineer Roland Pike questioned the decision of his boss Bert Hopwood, who wanted to do so solely with the works all-alloy A7 500 twins. These twins' top speed of 116mph shaded the '54 works Gold Stars at 114. Pike persuaded Hopwood to let the two machines do a drag run over a mile at MIRA with a 20mph flying start, reminding Bert that in racing, torque also matters. Sure enough, Pike on the Goldie crossed the line first; and the Goldie did it again after Pike had swapped machines with the other rider, racer David Tye. Hopwood took four of each machine to Daytona that year, and BSA twins came first and second, but with Gold Stars third, fourth and fifth. For 1956 it was second, third, fourth and fifth for the singles.

With its aura of brute, uncompromising power, the DBD34 walked it like it talked it.

BORN TO RUN

The pre-war genesis of the Gold Star ohv singles is well known. Retired TT winner Wal Handley's 1937 Brooklands 107.47mph lap on a methanol-fuelled Empire Star, winning a Brooklands Gold Star, was

One Gold Star ancestor, the 1938 M24..

"If you're going to have a Gold Star, you're going to have to ride."

followed by the 1938 production M24 Gold Star 500. Despite its alloy top end, because of BSA management's insistence that their sports machines should resemble the roadsters as much as possible, the M24 was pushed to top 85mph.

The real link with the post-war Goldies came not from designer Val Page's M-Series, but from the other string to his BSA bow, the B-Series, in the form of the highly tuned iron-engine 1939/40 B29 Silver Sports 350. Just 12 prototypes were built in 1939, and then much of the manufacturing equipment for the B29 was lost in the war. But surviving engines were used as early as 1947 for the development of the Gold Star, prior to its release for the 1949 model year as the ZB32 350.

The B29 had been a 350, which is why the post-war Goldie started in that capacity only. Also the large majority of demand for sporting BSA models at the time was for use in trials, extremely popular just after the war; 350 ohv singles were the weapon of choice in the feet-up game. But even BSA's ace works riders couldn't do too well on the rigid, iron-engined B32 competition models. The management policy of staying as close to the mass-produced roadsters as possible meant that these were lumbered with heavy steel tanks, mudguards, stays and brake back-plates, as well as a camel-like frame designed for use with

girder forks.

BSA's secret weapon in the Gold Star story was Irishman Bill Nicholson, a true all-rounder like the machine he helped to shape. Following consistent success in Ireland in most off-road events, on his much-modified girder-forked 350 pre-war B24, he

Yorkshire work ace and TV scrambles star Arthur Lampkin again, aviating a late Gold Star scrambler. Competition like this built in toughness for the Goldie.

Lucas Altette horn, magdyno, remote float chamber for Amal GP carb and shortened brake pedal to suit rear-sets.

was recruited at the end of 1946 by BSA Competitions chief Bert Perrigo, and given a new B32. After dismissing the latter ("useless compared to mine. The engine had no low-down poke and the steering angles were all wrong"), he was allowed to fit his own bike with BSA teles, and immediately won the prestigious Colmore Trial. Persuaded to contest his first-ever scramble, the Cotswold, on the ferry crossing over to

The Gold Star also excelled at Trials, even the toughest like this 1958 Scott Trial.

England he fitted his bike with a McCandless swinging-arm conversion. This was derided at the scramble, until Nicholson won the 350 class by a lap and a half, and proceeded to victory in the 500 and unlimited classes too.

At that event he met and got along very well with BSA Comp shop engineer and cam wizard Jack Amott, who made sure that Nicholson not only joined the BSA works team, but was also given the job of helping develop the sports model. It was they who dug out the B29 engines, added the M24's alloy top end and short 88mm stroke, and came up with a winning 350. To underline both his and the bike's versatility, Nicholson was entered, on a machine thus engined, for the 1947 Manx Grand Prix. Though he missed his refuelling stop and didn't feature in the results, the 350's performance proved that it had a future as a prospective road racer.

However, the sports model for 1949 was, strikingly, the first BSA production motorcycle with rear suspension – but it was by undamped plungers, cheaper and easier to produce than a full swinging-arm job. Dry weight was a claimed 378lbs, not light but not overweight. The model featured the Gold Star trademark, an alloy cylinder head and barrel, which saved 20lbs compared to the iron equivalent. But management voices at Small Heath had meant that the head was not the B29's racing type, but a sand-cast alloy version rmore suited to trials, with restrictions to port angles and sizes, valve angles and sizes, as well as to the combustion chamber shape, plus a shallow 7-degree downdraught angle. The cylinder head and rocker boxes were cast as one.

The inlet port's small (1-inch) diameter, suitable for trials work, could be machined out to 1⅟₁₆-inch to take an Amal 10 TT carb for scrambles, fast touring and racing versions, but the small valve sizes were restrictive. There was also a weakness in the design of the rather high-crowned piston, with a vulnerable thinness of the material between the bottom corner of the valve pocket and the top piston ring groove, mainly necessitated by the wide angle between the valves.

Despite these limitations, in its first year, 1949, a 350 Gold Star ridden by Harold Clarke went back to the Island and won the Junior Clubmans TT for the first of eight times. And the same year Nicholson on a plunger-sprung works Goldie scrambler won the I.o.M. Grand National – though, in one of several bits of rule-bending, his plungers featured one of his own inventions, a pair of hydraulic dampers within the standard-looking units. (Other pieces of non-standard naughtiness would include lighter frames, sometimes in Reynolds 531, for works trials and favoured works-

Swept-back exhaust, and carb bell-mouth big enough to suck in your trousers.

On parade. British Army team for the 1951 ISDT in Italy, led by future Goldie specialist Capt Eddie Dow (left), who won a Gold medal.

test of a ZB32, in both touring and Clubmans TT trim, recorded top speeds respectively of 78mph (5mph faster than a B31, and with better acceleration) and 90-plus for the Clubmans on open pipes, though it was noted that with the use of racing cams there was a loss of all power below 4000 rpm – in other words it was not suitable for road use.

If there was one word which summed up the Gold Star, it was versatility. From the first, many engine and trim options were offered, in pursuit of the ideal of a machine which could be used daily, then ridden to events at weekends, and with minimal work converted into a competitive mount. There were different sets of internal gearbox ratios to choose from, standard, scrambles and racing, plus a range of engine, gearbox and clutch sprockets. Several compression ratios were offered: 6.5:1 for touring and trials, 7.5:1 for racing on 75 octane Pool fuel, 8.0:1 for Clubmans and scramblers, with 8.8:1 for the latter using a 50/50 Benzol/petrol mix, and 9.0:1 or 13:1 for racing, the latter on methanol. There was a range of camshafts, and it was relatively easy to change them without having to dismantle the engine, as they rotated on fixed posts pressed into the crankcase, unlike the pre-war keyed type. And to alter the valve timing, access to the distinctive timing case was simple.

Gold Stars were always something special, and one thing that made them so was the price! A ZB32GS cost £211 for 1949 – with a speedo a fiver extra! –

One of the best drum brakes, BSA's single-sided 8-inch single leading shoe, preferred by many over the 190mm alternative.

supported Clubmans TT riders and scramblers; the clue would be their bronze welding.)

In trials, among much other success, Nicholson won the Scott Trial and in 1951 John Draper took the Scottish Six Days. The ZB34GS 500s meanwhile had been added for 1950, with the 350's 71 x 88mm dimensions bored out to 85 x 88mm, and the drive side inner roller main bearing increased in size. Already 500s had been supplied to the Army and BSA teams for the 1949 ISDT, and proved their robustness by taking 10 Golds.

This set the pattern, with the production 350 generally a year ahead of the 500 in engine development, until 1954/55 when the spotlight would fall firmly on the larger machines. A 1949 *Motor Cycling*

when a 350 Ariel Red Hunter was £147. By 1952 the ZB32GS cost £242, where a B31 roadster was £167. By 1960 the DBD34 500 Clubmans cost £307 11s, against Triumph's T120 650 Bonneville at £284 13s.

PATIENT DEVELOPMENT

What you were paying for began with the fact that Gold Stars in the early Fifties were individually assembled from selected parts, with one or two mechanics building each machine. After 1952, demand meant that Goldies were assembled on the regular production line – and according to the talented but independent-minded development engineer Roland Pike, many then had to be completely rebuilt! BSA at that time still made their own pistons, and Gold Star ones were manufactured to a high standard, the skirt machined with an industrial diamond giving a mirror-like finish, and the crown turned to a high finish and then polished. The flywheels were soon of a different shape to the B31/B33, and also polished, as were the crankcase, the ports and the con rod. Every Gold Star engine was dynamometer-tested for power, and a Certificate of Performance, showing bhp and torque, was presented to the owner.

Beneath all this was Val Page's strong, reliable engine design, benefitting from his prior experience working on Ariel and Triumph singles. The built-up crankshaft turned on main bearings consisting of drive side ball-race outer plus an inner roller, and a timing side roller. The crankcase was further stiffened with the addition of internal ribs, and a wider external rib around the periphery of the case, linking all the bosses securing the case to the frame. The 3-piece crankshaft with its initially 8-inch pressed-on flywheel could prove the Achilles heel for later super-tuned 500 racers, but was rarely a problem on the road. Four

Gold Star was a bike you really could ride to events, slap on race plates and foam rubber for 'chinning it', and ride competitively..

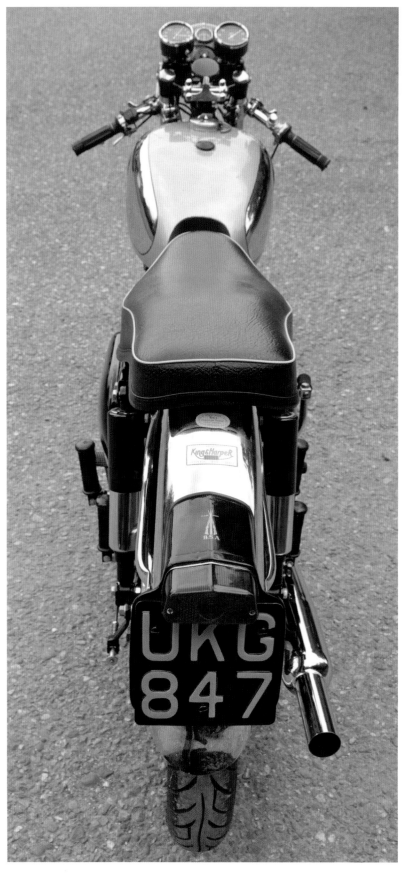

through-bolts secured the head rigidly to the barrel, screwing into the underside of the head and attached by special anchorages to the crankcase. Four more bolts, spaced between the through-bolts, independently secured the head to the barrel.

BSA metallurgy was then the finest in the industry, benefitting everything from the quality of the austenitic iron which lined the alloy barrel with its separate pushrod tubes, to the piston rings, and the hardening of components by Small Heath's own carbo-nitriding process which gave a .04-inch depth of extreme hardness on camshafts, etc. The sprawling Small Heath factory complex had its own forge, which produced work of a very high order; Roland Pike wrote, "I believe the forged steel con rods in BSA engines were outstandingly good." In Australia, where Gold Stars would dominate competition for the decade, the BSA rods had also been used successfully in ohc Manx Norton racers. Combine this with the in-house skills available like pipe-bending and gear-cutting, and it can be seen that the Gold Star represented the sum of everything that was good about BSA.

A final factor was the look. With black cycle parts

Beautiful from any angle. And LOUD!

Chrome rear chainguard was a Gold Star feature. The gap betwen the tyre and rear mudguard permitted the choice of bigger tyres for US competition.

Thing of beauty. Clip-ons, "twittering" silencer, folding rear-set so the over-centre kickstart can clear it – this DBD34 ticks all the boxes.

Gold Star's butterfly filler cap, breather pipe and big badge were all its own. Separate headlamp permitted twin Chronometric instruments. Clip-ons made sense at speed.

topped by that chromed petrol tank with maroon-lined, frosted silver panels bearing the iconic Gold Star transfers, and later, big red round plastic badges, plus chrome for the mudguards and stays, for the fork spring covers, rear chainguard, and brake back-plates, this was a handsome, eager-looking machine.

1952 was a significant change year for the ZB32/ZB34. There was a major engine revision, some of which had first been found on the 500s from late 1951. The cylinder head, for production reasons now die-cast not sand-cast, was completely redesigned, with the rocker boxes now separate and nine studs holding the boxes to the head for rigidity. The valve angles were reduced and no longer symmetrical , and the downdraught angle increased to a more efficient 15 degrees. The inlet port was reshaped to give a tapered venturi (fireman's nozzle) form. The valves themselves featured a smaller head size for the inlet one, combined with a larger head size for the exhaust.

Development chief Bert Hopwood had gone to the Daytona Beach races in 1951 and witnessed multiple Gold Star failures of the gearbox, valves and rocker gear. Broken exhaust valves, with the stems breaking at the sharp corner of the groove, had been a principal problem. Re-finishing them, plus the use of proprietary Bullock split cotters for the valve guides, and in April, quietening ramps on the camshafts to let the valve down on its seat more progressively, were all

Gold Star at speed down Bray Hill for the Manx Grand Prix.

Ultimate Tower of Power. Final, heavily finned DBD34 engine, with characteristic swept-back exhaust, the heart of this late 500 Goldie in Clubmans trim.

partial solutions.

However, according to Pike, re-shaping the valve was what solved it, with the underside of the valve head now blending into the stem with a long taper portion, and the shape changed, with the "tulip head" of the valve reduced to a small saucer. In mid-year, for the Clubmans models, the valve steel also changed to a superior alloy, Nimonic 80. In another example of BSA's advantages as a self-sufficient industrial giant, this material had been sourced from elsewhere in the Group, where it was being used for the manufacture of turbine blades; it would set an industry standard. The austenitic iron valve seats changed from screw-in to shrunk-in, with shorter, pressed-in valve guides in Hidurel 5.

The upper part of the pushrod tunnel, which was now cast-in, was finned horizontally, with the "piled arms" insignia on its cover now in relief rather than engraved. The new cylinder head permitted the use of 8.0:1 pistons, lighter than the previous ones, with a crown less raised, a reduced stiffening rib and thinned-down walls. With the piston's skirt length reduced by ¼ inch, scoops were added to clear the flywheel at BDC. The piston's compression rings were changed from ³⁄₃₂-inch wide L-section to ¹⁄₁₆-inch plain; this reduced pressure on the cylinder walls and the previous danger of scuffing. All this meant that the previous danger point at the bottom of the piston's valve pocket was eliminated. The 350's connecting rod was now ½ inch shorter, as Pike had found that

this increased performance by reducing inertia loadings; so there was one less barrel fin. The engine breathing was also revised.

What all this amounted to were engines more fitted for speed work, in scrambles and racing. The popularity of trials had begun to wane, and BSA management now thought that it was speed events, like the first Senior/Junior Clubmans TT double victory for the Goldies in 1954, which sold machines. As the man overseeing development, the great designer Bert Hopwood wrote that Managing Director James Leek "issued demands that BSA products were second to none in production racing, trials and scrambles."

Every step of the Gold Star's development had been marked by clashes with management – sometimes including, surprisingly, Bert Hopwood. As Roland Pike wrote, Hopwood said "the 500 Gold Star was obsolete anyway, and not to worry ourselves about [an improved piston ring]. The twin was the thing now." In fact Hopwood, with the admirable aim of planning for the future, was conceiving, as he wrote, his revolutionary but ill-fated 250 MC1 monoshock racers as "a new generation of Gold Star machines."

Nevertheless, it was in the Development shop which Hopwood had demanded as a condition of his

employment that the painstaking work, some already detailed, was carried out, which would result in the ultimate DBD34. The following account is not exhaustive and concentrates on the 500. Meanwhile, conflicts remained. Hopwood found a pretext to fire Jack Ammott, whom he told me had been briefing against him weekly to James Leek "on what I was doing wrong" about the MC1, and shortly afterwards

Clubmans Gold Star riding position took no prisoners.

Goldie for export: West Coast 500 with high bars, small gas tank.

Bill Nicholson resigned in exasperation. Hopwood added that "Pike had a temper too, he'd just as soon throw a hammer at you."

1953 brought the BB models, the first swinging-arm BSAs, with a modified version of Nicholson's frame. As Pike described, Bill Nicholson, who once tested a new trials frame by riding it up and down the main staircase at the factory, "was forever trying new (steering) head angles…and it proved a job to tie him down to a final set-up." However, after the Drawing

Office had added the necessary roadster attachments and altered the head angle slightly for road use, the frame which would feature on BSA roadster twins and singles for the next 18 years made its debut on the Goldie.

All-welded, with duplex downtubes, the sturdy chassis also carried the "A" gearbox as developed by Hopwood for the twins. A robust design with some resemblance to the Triumph box, it was offered with a wide variety of ratios suiting trials, scrambles, racing, touring and US competition. Its only weak spot under road racing conditions would prove to be the layshaft bushes. Development found an answer via the use of Torrington needle roller bearings; in the ultimate incarnation, the RRT2 box offered as an option from 1956 on, with the "RR" for extra close ratio, the "T" indicated Torrington, while the "2" signified that they were used at both ends of the layshaft as on the RRT, but also on the mainshaft sleevegear, as well as involving a higher first gear than the RRT. On the Gold Star, the box's newly designed shell pivoted to tension the primary chain, rather than being drawn directly to the rear as previously.

Petrol tanks with convenient single centre-bolt fixings featured, the 5½-pint oil tank was rubber-mounted, and there was provision on the Gold Star version of the frame for mounting folding rear-set footrests for Clubmans and other racing; as well as extra gusseting featured around the steering head. In common with the B31/B33 roadster singles, the frame was kinked outward on the right-side lower rail to clear the pre-unit engine's protuberant oil pump. The Goldie's frame was also constructed from the same grade of tubing as the roadsters', the only significant difference being the lugs applicable to the type of competition the sports single would be used for, and the extra headstock gusseting (the exceptions as mentioned being the odd "special" frame in Reynolds 531).

The hinge in the Gold Star story, when the 350 was displaced by the 500 on the cutting edge of development and as the ultimate icon, began in the winter of 1953. A more heavily finned cylinder head was planned for the 350, along with changes to the piston and crankpin, and Bert Hopwood persuaded MD James Leek that it would not cost much more to produce the big square-finned head for the 500 too. Designed by Brian Jones in the Drawing Office, consulting daily with Pike, this was the genesis of the CB series produced from April 1954 for the Clubmans variants, and as Pike commented, "The 1954 Gold Star engine was almost a new engine, it had the same bore and stroke but not much else," much of which was due to the Development department's patient work. The new head featured fins sloped between the two rocker box joints, to get air across "dead space" on top of the head, as well as much increased horizontal cooling fin area on head and barrel.

Some Goldies had previously suffered from blown head gaskets and burnt cylinder combustion chambers; this was effectively sorted by the novel use of Plexal-peelable layered gaskets (though there was a potential penalty with this product, where you peel

Chuck Minnert aviates his Goldie on his way to winning at Catalina 1956.

the layers off till you have the thickness required; owners tended to get the head gasket too thin, until the head was sitting on the iron cylinder liner, with the tension then stressing the alloy head and making it prone to cracks.) The cylinder head porting was completely redesigned. The use of stronger valve springs, W and S American ones, originally provided by BSA's West Coast man Hap Alzina, cured previous problems in that area and helped provide a substantial increase in maximum revs. The downdraught angle of the inlet port became better still, which sprang from an early interim works adaptation of the 350 head for the 500.

The weight of the valve gear had put a big load on the valves, a stress which had been an inhibiting factor previously. On the new head the gear was lightened by the use of eccentric rocker spindles for adjustment purposes. The valve spring collars also changed to lighter Duralumin, and the collet seat angle was increased. The 500's con rod was now shortened, like the 350's, with this year's 500 flywheels being oval to

Typical race-modified Goldie, with 5-gallon fibreglass petrol tank, central oil tank, ventilated twin leading shoe front brake, home-brewed rear-set controls and open mega.

Modified DBD34 with goodies including alloy tank plus Dow 'Duetto' front brake, and nickel-plated frame.

permit the piston to clear the forged steel flywheel at BDC. The pushrods, also shortened, had changed from solid Dural with steel caps riveted on, to hollow T4 alloy tubing with lighter end caps pressed on.

As mentioned, the engine's breathing was also modified, from the previous small pen steel discs, which at high speeds had allowed too much oil to blow out, sometimes draining the tank and getting on the rear wheel. Now a mechanical breather, a rotating sleeve in the timing cover driven by a peg off the magneto, successfully cured this. An Amal GP carburettor with a flexibly-mounted float chamber was fitted for the first time.

The bottom end of the 350 fell in line with the 500, with its timing side crankcase stiffened internally, and the 500's larger timing side main roller bearing, with its modified lubrication, fitted. 350s were now giving 33-34bhp, but it was the 38-40bhp 500s which grabbed the 1954 glory, beating the ohc Norton Internationals to win the Senior Clubmans TT for the first time and make it the first of three Senior/Junior

double victories for the Goldies. After 1956, when 53 out of the 55 starters in the Senior were Gold Star mounted, the event was discontinued on the Island and the focus shifted to Production races like Thruxton.

From then on for fast road use, for Rockers it had to be a 500. "The 350 was perhaps a nicer bike to ride on the road," said Dow's mechanic John Gleed, "but despite what's been said, it had nowhere near the power of a 500," and latter-day specialist Phil Pearson added that "the 350 may be the stronger motor but it's not very powerful." Nevertheless at Thruxton in 1956 it was, sensationally, the 350 ridden by Ivor Lloyd/Ken Jones which won overall, establishing Gold Star domination of the event until 1958. The same went for trials and particularly scrambles, while in America a Gold Star had won at the tough 100-mile dirt-and-tarmac course on Catalina Island in 1951, and they took 1st, 2nd and 3rd there in 1956, providing the Catalina name for the US scrambles Goldie – "the world's most successful scrambler."

1955 brought the DB models for Clubmans or racing machines, with the 500's flywheels turned down and reverting to round, and its piston's skirts shortened; according to Roland Pike, this was because Production did not like doing the unusual oval ones. Pike believed the turned-down round ones made the engine less smooth, "but riders liked them" so they were adopted. The diameter of the valve springs and collets became smaller, while the GP carb became larger, with its float chamber support changed to a vertical mounting, and the cylinder head's inlet tract lengthened. Experiments had shown that using a larger carb gained power, but that it was lost again if the inlet port was opened out to match. So the venturi in the tract already mentioned continued in use. The oil feed to the big end now incorporated an oil seal in the timing cover, as the pressure feed via a quill in the rcrankshaft was reversed; and the big end crankpin and cage were modified to reduce wear.

Visually the biggest innovation for the 1955 Clubmans were the new exhaust and silencer. The exhaust length had been shortened, by sweeping it back across the cylinder, to suit the silencer, whose internals were in two parts – a megaphone shape, with the silencer's front "shoulders" externally reduced to a conical shape, and a small expansion chamber followed by a short, straight-through absorption silencer. Increased ground clearance when cornering was an additional benefit.

1956 saw the ultimate version emerge for Clubmans and racing models, the DBD34, with a few refinements. Clubmans TT regulations had altered to require both a silencer and lighting equipment. The latter was coped with by fitting a rear-mounted Lucas Magdyno with manual advance/retard control; the former by Pike adapting 1955's effort to a variation known as the "twittering" silencer due to its metallic chirping sound on the over-run, caused by the extractor action of the silencer plus a large degree of valve overlap. Thus a street-legal racer was born. The 500-only DBD's GP carb grew to 1½ inches, and was mounted to a further modified cylinder head. The RRT2 gearbox was introduced, as were the optional alloy 5-gallon Lyta petrol tank, and the 190mm front brake.

Gold Star brakes had long been special, featuring since 1950 six ventilation holes in the single-sided 8-inch front one's backplate, blanked off by detachable plugs until they were needed on track. Late in 1955 the 7-inch QD rear brake had changed to the "Alfin" type, a finned light alloy casting bonded into position and also with six ventilating holes. The 8-inch single leading shoe front brake, modified for 1955 with three extra cooling fins, was very good of its type, but as outputs rose, the need was felt for a better one. Unfortunately it was decreed that it had to suit both racers and scramblers, and as Pike recounted, Dennis Hardwicke in the Comp. shop wanted a smaller brake for the off-roaders, while Pike's colleague, TT rider Charlie Salt, wanted a big one for the Clubmans. Charlie suggested the 190mm diameter, "banking on a belief that Hardwicke would not know how big 190mm really was" – it was 7.48 inches, and Hardwicke didn't. The brake, in a full-width hub with 2-inch wide linings, was criticized by some as spongy, though John Gleed qualified that as "often down to the cable – you need a really heavy-gauge one" like the factory originals at that time. The 190mm formed the basis of Eddie Dow's excellently effective twin leading shoe "Duetto" conversions, but of the original equipment, Pike felt that "the earlier cast-iron [single-sided 8-inch] drum with ribs around it – that was the best Gold Star brake."

These many developments may have made tedious reading, but they resulted in a 500 single with power increased from 1952's 37bhp to 1956's 44-46bhp on the best ones and 42 as standard for the Clubmans, with top speeds in excess of 110mph as well as impressive speeds in the tall gears – including over 100 in third. The increase stemmed from the higher revs, up to a safe limit of 7000rpm, made possible by the lighter valve gear, shorter con rods, better valve springs, larger carbs, higher compression, and cooler running from the big fins and higher octane fuel.

And at that point in 1956, all factory development virtually ceased. Hopwood had departed to head Norton in Spring 1955, while Pike remained to see the 1956 boardroom revolution in which BSA Group

Phil Pearson and his DBD-mounted crew walk it like they talk it.

Chairman Sir Bernard Docker was displaced by the former owner of Triumph, Jack Sangster, at which point Pike departed for SU Carburettors. He felt, like more than one BSA executive, that Triumph's Edward Turner, whom Sangster soon put in charge of the BSA Automotive Division, of which Triumph since 1952 had been a part, would see the tough single as a threat to his sports Tiger 100 twins, which it had trounced at the Clubmans TT.

Development duly stopped, but the Goldie's popularity saved it, especially in the States where its exceptional ruggedness continued to be appreciated by sports-oriented riders used to destroying Britain's offerings in short order. Some Stateside dealers were said to have threatened to refuse to take their stock of BSA twins unless they were accompanied by a quota

Clip-on bars punished your wrists – but not at speed.

of Gold Stars. The 350s were discontinued after 1958, though they could still be had to special order. Probably never more than 2000 Goldies, if that, were built per year, and the majority, before the end came at the beginning of 1963, were DBD34s. Reduced from 1957 to scramblers and Clubmans only, the catalogue stated that the Clubmans "specification is such that it is neither intended nor suitable for road use as a touring motorcycle." But boys will be boys, and the Rockers scarcely had touring in mind.

NO SURRENDER

As you will have gathered, big Gold Stars were not the easiest machines to live with, though if you managed it the rewards were considerable. Your charismatic machine looked great, handled and steered very well, at the top end could hold high speeds for longer, and eventually could see off almost all the opposition. But there were downsides; you lost out to twins getting away, the ride could be harsh and loud, and pitfalls abounded.

The first hurdle was starting. "The Goldie was fine for the road," said John Gleed, "if three things were seen to: a good magneto; the carburation right; and knowing the starting drill. The biggest mistake was if you'd retarded the ignition a bit, and it kicked back, to then retard it fully – that was hopeless. And you didn't want too wide a plug gap – the book says 18 to 20, but I always set mine at 15. Dow set the Gold Stars we sold up right, including us giving them a test ride. We never had any coming back after a month saying they couldn't cope."

Assuming a good magneto, the GP carb absolutely should not be over-flooded prior to starting, and it lacked a reliable tickover setting. Other difficulties were the way its extended open bell-mouth could suck

your trouser leg in on the move, and how, parked up, you had to stuff its gaping mouth with a rag or a bath-plug in case of rain. Running, it was temperature sensitive, fluffing in the cold, and revs had to be kept at a healthy level, above 3000rpm. In traffic, throttle finesse was necessary; if you just wound the throttle off, you found yourself floundering in an unpleasant lumpiness which it took a long time, and probably a down-change, to recover from, with the threat of stalling and the unpleasantness of a hot start always hovering in the wings. Compared to a twin, tiny progressive increments of throttle change were the thing, rather than big handfuls, to keep revs up and husband the power.

The starting drill was the same as for other big singles, but the engine's aura of brute, uncompromising power was not deceptive, and with 9.0:1 compression or more, at the end of the drill another element was necessary – as one owner put it, "You've got to give them a good welt. A lot of people aren't aggressive enough with them."

On the move, the DBD was relatively light at 365lbs, but with clip-ons the steering felt heavy at low speed. The gear pedal could be awkward to reach from the rear-sets. You suffered from the clip-on/rear-sets riding position in traffic, but it made perfect sense as the road opened out, speeds rose and the wind on your chest took the weight off your wrists, leaving you well-balanced, with your weight forward where it should be, and aboard a reassuringly solid-feeling machine which handled reliably and steered extremely precisely. You needed commitment to corner fast in that riding position, but if you had it, the Gold Star would not let you down.

One handling proviso was voiced by café racer Mike

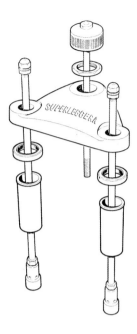

Eddie Dow's "Superleggera" front fork internal conversion.

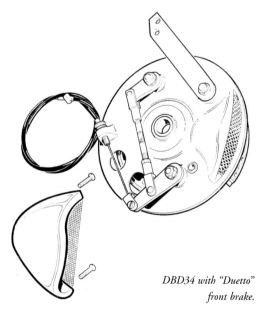

Eddie Dow's "Duetto" twin leading shoe front brake conversion.

DBD34 with "Duetto" front brake.

Clay, a Goldie veteran, who wrote, "The steering head…is high, and this in turn dictates fork stanchions of a length that will magnify the whip inherent in all conventional [telescopic] fork designs," adding that with the BSA fork's rebound-only damping, which famously makes it clang on full extension, a series of bumps could make it bottom out, with "interesting" consequences on high-speed bends. He found Eddie Dow's Superleggera double-damping conversion the complete answer, but this does reduce the 3 inches of front suspension movement to 2, making for a harsh ride.

The need for clutch-slipping was mentioned at the start, but once on the move, at 70 in top the engine was hardly working at all, and you were at the bottom of an endless and endlessly steepening power curve. This unstoppable feeling of power accumulating with each detonation, and carrying on and on far further up the scale than most, defined the Goldie as an ultimate single. It did take its time to get to ton-plus speeds in top, and the 500 Velocette was far more civilised and tractable. There were hard shakes through the Goldie's bars from 3500 to 4000 revs, and the exhaust is a very loud, flat roar (but only a silencer with the correct internals, not just the shape, would release the Goldie's power). Overtaking, you didn't whip round cars as you would have on a twin, you hammered your way past. Goldies have a unique, muscular appeal. As I once wrote, "If this bike was a county, it would be Yorkshire. Gritty, uncompromisingly masculine, no-nonsense; it delivers, and goes on delivering, in a crunch." You can see why the minority who did choose them often found that after that, nothing else would do.

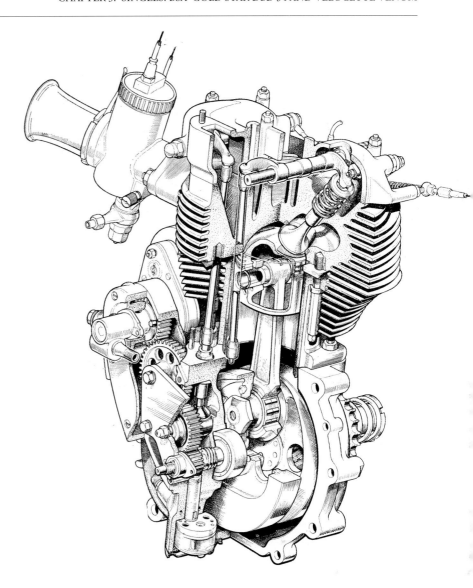

The author let loose on a Pearson Goldie.

TECHNICAL SPECIFICATIONS:
1957 BSA DBD34 GOLD STAR CLUBMANS

Capacity	499cc
Bore	85mm
Stroke	88mm
Compression	9.0:1
Power output	42bhp@7000rpm
Electrical system	6 volt
Ignition	Magneto
Generator	Dynamo
Wheels and tyres	F: 3.00x19. R:3.25x19
Brakes	F: 8-inch. R: 7-inch
Weight (dry)	380lbs
Max speed	110mph

VELOCETTE VENOM

"There was a guy called Buckley at Johnson's café with a very fast Velocette Viper. It had a high compression piston and some mild port tuning and it went like a rocket. Unfortunately he was wiped out by Clearways up on the straight at Brands Hatch by a Citroen DS who decided to treat it like a three-lane highway."

Harry Winch, ex-AMC worker.

Space only allows a very brief look at the black and gold singles from Hall Green, Birmingham. High-priced and made in small numbers, their old-fashioned appearance should have excluded them as a choice for young riders. But their race breeding, their unexpectedly good handling, and the firm's justified reputation for the fine engineering embodied in their design and construction, were recognised, and tales of quick Velos in the café mix were surprisingly common, even though their fastest incarnation, the 1965-on Thruxton Venom, lies outside our period.

Of journalist Dave Minton's hard-riding weekend group of Essex friends in the early Sixties, he found that among the touring motorcycles of the time, only two could consistently stand the all-day, sometimes 90mph-plus pace. One was a BSA A10 650 with an Avon Streamliner fairing, and the other a Venom

Clubman, "which while unable to overtake the rasping twins, was impossible to leave behind."

The 500 Venom, and its equally effective sibling the 350 Viper, were introduced for 1956, developed from an ill-fated US-originated 500 Scrambler, and from tuning work on the previous 500 MSS by Reg Orpin at London Velo specialists L. Stevens. The 36bhp Venom adopted the MSS engine's square dimensions of 86 x 86mm, while the 27bhp Viper's were new, being a sleeved-down Venom, and thus relatively long-stroke at 72 x 86mm. This made it the livelier, revvier engine, capable of bursts at 7000rpm, while the Venom was a steadier single, topping out just above 6000rpm. Top speed for the 350 was 92mph, and for the Venom at least 102mph, with one road test on a Clubmans machine, with the optional TT9 carb, recording 110mph. The ton-up performance was achieved

Timeless, race-bred looks. A Venom could keep up with the pack. This example is a Clubman MkII from 1967.

with the use of a high (4.4:1) top gear, yet the Velo singles remained remarkably tractable.

On the plus side, a Venom in traditional gold-lined black (there were unfortunate two-tone options) with chromed mudguards and sometimes chrome tank panels, looked good. Although the "fish-tail" silencer was undeniably antique, a genuine one was absolutely necessary for optimum performance, and it gave a deep mellow exhaust note which rose to "a roar you could stand on" at speed. The "arcuate" adjustment of the rear units with their curved upper slots could also look odd.

The all-alloy engine was slung low in a frame made of top Reynolds 531 tubing, but traditionally constructed by pinning and brazing rather than welding, with the large malleable iron lugs which sleeved the frame around its mounting points making it strong but heavy. The swinging-arm was unusual in featuring two tapered legs, each independently

Old-fashioned looking but still a contender – the Venom could go the high-speed distance better than many.

1956 Venom with chrome tank panels.

attached. You could move these by hand, yet the steering and high-speed handling were judged by Titch Allen to be "pluperfect."

The narrow engine featured a single camshaft, driven via an idler gear, which was set high in the timing chest, behind its distinctive "Map of India" cover. The engines were mechanically quiet, being built to fine limits, and with expensive helically-cut timing gears rather than the usual straight-cut kind, and belt rather than chain drive to the forward-mounted dynamo. Ignition was by rear-mounted

magneto, either BTH or Lucas, manually controlled for the 1960-on Clubmans versions.

The unusual taper-roller main bearings with taper bores were carried right up close to the flywheels, making for an exceptionally smooth single. They were a demanding, precision job to set up, with the vital correct pre-load achieved by shimming; so not an easy job for the home mechanic. They were however very robust and long-lived. The narrow gearbox in its square casing featured gears engaging via internal dogs, and power going in on the sleeve gear and out

1958 Venom on test.

Velocette handling was legendary, despite the flimsy-seeming swinging-arm

Beautiful late Venom Clubman.

on the mainshaft, the opposite of normal Brit practice. But the box was very strong, and with high, close ratios for the Venom, provided one of the best and smoothest of changes.

The 16-spring clutch was more problematic, being mounted inboard of the final drive sprocket to keep the width down. There was nothing fundamentally wrong with a device featured on a machine which won its classes in long-distance races like the 1957 Bol D'Or, or which, after a hairy session at Montlhéry in

Venom Clubman was for serious riders, and could handle serious distances at high speeds.

1961, set a world record averaging 100.5mph for 24 hours. But clutch adjustment was different from others – Velo owners always carried a ¼-inch steel rod to poke through the sprocket's holes and tighten the clutch – and plate clearances were small because of the lack of space, so perfectly flat plates, and all components in top condition, were a must. And the clutch would not stand abuse.

Other downsides were: oil leaks, particularly from the primary chaincase; rapid wet-sumping when stood, despite a ball-valve in the oil-feed union to stop oil draining when cold; relatively high weight at around 380lbs, when Triumph twins could be 20lbs lighter; and a Miller electrical system including a troublesome regulator which lacked capacity. One Velo owner returning from a trip to Russia reported proudly that his lights had worked perfectly all the way. A fellow owner responded curiously, "How could you tell?" A final irritant was difficult starting, aggravated by very low ratio kickstart gearing. A good mag, "the drill", and the famous long swinging kick were all necessary.

Riding one was a rare mixture of civilised and speedy. The well-sprung Venom was very comfortable,

Original 1967 Venom Clubman MkII.

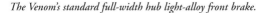

The Venom's standard full-width hub light-alloy front brake.

Twinned instruments and manual advance/retard but standard bars – most Velocettes ended up different

Fishtail silencer was a must to release Velo single's power.

Gearchange linkage and fold-up rear-set footpeg.

Final, potent development, the 1965-on Venom Thruxton

"Map of India" timing chest and high-cam engine were unique. This one's carburettor is from much later.

seat included, though the seat height was quite tall. In stark contrast to the Goldie, the engine was extremely tractable and unfussy, it could be trickled at low revs and then pull away smoothly, again and again, with narrow flywheels making for good acceleration. The steering and roadholding were completely precise,

second only to a Norton, and the bike came alive at speed. Alternative biking guru Royce Creasey wrote of his Venom, "The funny thing is that although [the rear frame] all moves about over bumps, and if the front wheel hits anything big enough to lift it you'll probably get a couple of flicks from the steering, it never gets off-line."

The Venom's stock full-width hub light alloy brakes, 7½-inch front, 7-inch rear, were effective. Performance goodies were readily available from specialists, and the Clubmans versions from 1960 carried several of them as standard. The province of enthusiasts, and almost bespoke, of the 6750 Venoms built over a dozen years, probably no two ended up quite the same. They could be durable and reliable, but as Yorkshire dealer Wilf Green summed up these well-engineered but quirky machines, "The customer really did have to have an engineering background to accept the problems and enjoy an undoubted quality individualistic bike."

From the Ritz to the Ace, the Velocette single's timeless classic looks were never out of place.

TECHNICAL SPECIFICATIONS: 1958 VELOCETTE VENOM CLUBMANS

Capacity	499cc
Bore	86mm
Stroke	86mm
Compression	8.5:1
Power output	37bhp@6200rpm
Electrical system	6 volt
Ignition	Magneto
Generator	Miller DVR belt-driven dynamo
Wheels and tyres	F: 3.00x19. R: 3.50x19
Brakes	F: 8-inch. R: 7-inch
Weight (dry)	398lbs
Max speed	111.9mph

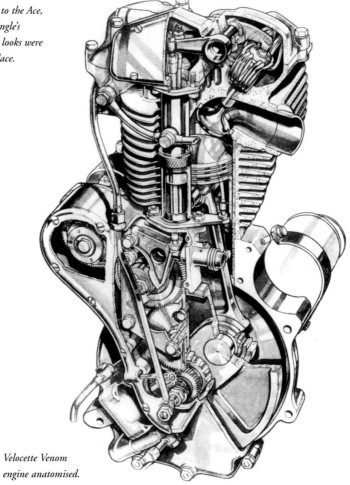

Velocette Venom engine anatomised.

CHAPTER 4:
TRIUMPH TIGER T110 AND T120 BONNEVILLE

TIGER T110

"Every summer morning I'd go through the village...on my '58 T110, at 80 to 90mph. And there was a shopkeeper there, a real character, stout, balding, who'd come out every day and shake his fist at me.
"Then one morning he was just stood there smiling, with his arms folded – and round the corner, a policeman stepped out. I told myself, you're gonna have to cam it, and knocked down a gear, gave it some throttle and rode round him. Then it was the copper who was shaking his fist! I did the seven miles to work with a cop car not far behind. I shot into the Dairy yard and spotted my mate Mick and his trailer truck with the hydraulic lift platform. We got the T110 up there and shut in the truck just as the cops arrived, and the guy on the gate covered for me. They searched the car park; that night and for the next four days, I got a lift home in a car, because that's how long they were waiting outside. I did use to ride that T110 hard..."

Kent-based Rocker Keith Avery

Triumph pre-unit 650 twins were at the centre of the Rocker cult, often the fastest, always the most numerous, the most economical, most tuneable and most lusted-after motorbikes of them all. They became more so as the movement swelled, catching its momentum with 1959's iconic T120 pre-unit Bonneville, which transformed itself over a four-year lifespan into the quintessence of speed and graceful flash, the bike that in 1960/61 could beat all others, straight from the crate. The pre-unit version's end, too, coincided with the waning of the hardcore Rockers' world after 1962.

Of course the cleverly redesigned '63-on unit versions were best-sellers too, and in some respects the better bike, but as ton-up boy Mike Clay wrote, "The 650s lost much of their charisma…Café racers everywhere hated [the unit Bonnie], though there were still plenty who were prepared to hock their soul on the never-never to buy one." Pre-units with their longer cases were the best engine to use in Tritons, and as another aficionado put it, they "had the class."

What was the secret of these twins' success? For a start, Triumph had got there first, with the '37-on Speed Twin. The pre-war sensation lingered on, and Edward Turner, like Jaguar's William Lyons, "knew what the public wanted before they knew it themselves" – affordable speed. Triumphs quickly became synonymous in the minds of riders with inexpensive,

reliable (didn't the Police use them?), easy to work on, fast but non-threatening machines, which if you wanted to go even faster, could be adapted to do so easily enough without breaking the bank.

Under Turner's benevolent dictatorship, the company, in its new-built wartime factory at Meriden outside Coventry, became streamlined by abandoning

Triumph style at its finest for 1954 T110.

Brochure page for 1954 T110.

Like all Triumph handlebars until 1963, these "Flanders" export bars were of 1-inch diameter (rather than the industry standard 7/8th inch). The control lever on the left side is manual advance/retard for the magneto on this sports model.

post-war everything but twins, and by commonising the different models as much as possible. The aim was to produce a range of motorcycles with universal appeal, being competitively priced, mechanically quiet, and smooth – this is hard to grasp today, after later Triumphs, and parallel twins in general, have become known for the opposite, but in the late Thirties, Forties and Fifties, compared with the jarring concussions of single-cylinder bikes, Triumph twins with the characteristic whir of their gear-driven transmission, timing and electrics, seemed positively

Parcel grid and styling bands offset Triumph's lack of chromed tanks.

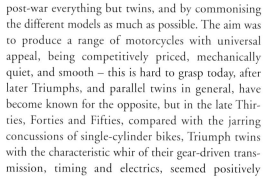

civilised. With low compression due to 72 octane Pool fuel, forgiving transmission, and aided perhaps by their crankshafts' freedom to flex, they purred along smoothly, as the rest of the industry played catch-up. There was always a waiting list for Triumphs.

None of this would have worked for long if in addition the engines had not been so lively. Of all the characteristics in a motorcycle, acceleration is perhaps the universally desirable one. The engine's use of Riley-type hemispherical combustion chambers contributed, but the late Titch Allen wrote, from experience, "The Triumph engine has periods of balance and periods of imbalance and it seems to have a natural tendency to seek out the calm periods… Triumph engines show in some subtle way that they are eager to go faster. Are spoiling for a scrap…eager to go singing up the scale." This inimitable eagerness was what hooked riders on Triumphs, despite their weaknesses in other areas.

A further element was the Triumphs' lightness. The 1957 T110 weighed 390lbs, against an equivalent BSA Road Rocket at 418lbs. "Add lightness and simplicate," they said at Meriden, though "the minimum of metal for the maximum of work" philosophy had its penalties, as with the Triumph front fork. But anyone can immediately appreciate lightness in a motorcycle, whether pushing it about or slinging it round a corner, while durability or the lack of it take time to emerge.

The 1954 Tiger 110. This very one on road test with Motor Cycling *topped 115 mph – in slightly dubious circumstances.*

Finally, in addition to affordable speed, Triumphs had style. Other UK factories at that time simply let form follow function, but artistic Mr Turner with his "pencil", draughtsman Jack Wickes, made conscious styling work for them. This was evident from the open-sided rear light housing that could double as a lifting handle, to the chrome surround of the elegant front number plate. The headlamp nacelle, routing the cables neatly and containing all the instruments previously found in a tank-top panel, was utterly characteristic, both shapely and, in combination with swept 1-inch diameter pullback handlebars,

Straight from the crate for 1954, the new Tiger T110, this one with US export bars.

1954 T110 sported Amal single carb with TT remote float chamber.

enhancing the impression of speed – even if Americans preferred a separate headlamp, and the nacelle enforced less than perfect cable runs as well as limiting headlight adjustment.

The chromed 1957-on "mouth-organ" tank badges, apparently based on the grilles of Buicks, encapsulated the burgeoning Anglo-American brashness of the late Fifties while still containing the classic curling script of the Triumph logo, and, in conjunction with short chromed median strips, separated the top and bottom of the tank to allow the use of the increasingly popular, eye-grabbing, two-tone colour schemes, with Triumph, unlike others, almost always getting the combinations right. Rockers in that pre-merchandise era used the badges as belt buckles.

HOT AND HOTTER

The sports 650 began for 1954 with the Tiger T110, which along with its Tiger T100 500cc sibling, introduced Triumph's first-ever swinging-arm frame. The "Ton-Ten" was a sensation straight out of the gate. That was despite the all-alloy engined T100 being the one for which most of the sporting optional extra equipment was made available, including a £30 racing kit incorporating a twin-carb conversion. That was due to the 500cc upper limit in most European sport, and the AMA-dictated one in US Class C racing.

Left: Scalloped-edge spoke flange on 8-inch front brake was for 1954 only.

Strong, versatile and fast, Triumph's 650 twin was the one. Spares suppliers loved the hex-headed rocker inspection caps for their tendency to unscrew and go AWOL.

"Teardrop" silencers were pretty and, unbaffled for the US, pretty loud.

In 1955 Rich Richards on a stripped, rigid Triumph 650 achieved a one-way run of 153.06 mph at Bonneville.

Little brother leads. 500cc US race-kitted T100 for 1957, complete with twin-carb kit.

The T110 650, however, was the essence of budget speed at £240, when its closest real rival, the Featherbed-framed version of Norton's Dominator, was still only a 500 and cost £19 more. BSA's A10 in its new swinging-arm frame was £27 cheaper, but it was the 6T Thunderbird's equivalent, as the iron-engined A10 couldn't top the ton, and the sportier Road Rocket version wouldn't be along in the UK for another two

and a half years. By that time the T110 had established itself as the cowboy's choice, as well as Triumph's sales leader in America. The fastest Ace café riders would run T110s, like "the King", Barry "Noddy" Cheese – "Boy did he make that thing move!" – and future Production racer Ron Wittich, though the latter was soon putting the Triumph engine in a Norton-framed special.

A big boost had come at the start, with a 1954 road test by *Motor Cycling* Editor Bernal Osborne, which strikingly had achieved, once the carb had been re-jetted, "a flash reading of 117.2mph." The late Triumph expert Hughie Hancox, then working in Meriden's Rectification department, later said that after Osborne had enjoyed a morning session with the bike in standard trim, Turner took the journalist

America First. Stylish 1957 US export race-kitted twin carb T100 Tiger 500.

to lunch while, unbeknownst to Osborne, Hancox and his fellows dismantled the engine, replaced the stock sports E3325 cams and followers with the famous US-derived high-performance E3134 cams and "R" followers, reset the timing and handed the twin back for the afternoon speed tests. Hughie, however, liked to spin a yarn, and John Nelson, author of the seminal book *Bonnie* and in charge of Rectification at the time, disputed that version, asserting that the engine was in that state prior to the road test, but what was added for the speed runs was a straight-through exhaust system which released the full power of the set-up.

But either way, the point was lodged with the speed-minded young that here was a twin with a top speed comfortably over 100mph, and the potential with tuning for more. The point would be hammered home in 1955 and '56 when at Bonneville Salt Flats, Johnny Allen took 650 Triumph stream-liners to world record speeds, sending what Hancox called "a great wave of euphoria [sweeping] through the factory," despite the fact that a) the records were disputed on a technicality, and b) the 650 had been based on an all-iron Thunderbird, much modified by Texas dealers Big D and with a twin-carb conversion, rather than on the T110 which by 1956 had an alloy cylinder head.

Bernal Osborne in 1954 had emphasized the 8.0:1 c.r. machine's flexibility (he had covered the on/off road ISDT in Wales on it prior to the test), and its excellent mpg (65-70 average). To his credit, Edward Turner was at pains to ensure that, in production tune, even his sports twins remained practical and useable (Osborne found the key to T110 docility in traffic was intelligent use of the manual advance/retard control provided on the magneto). Veteran journalist Bob Currie recalled the early T110s as noticeably harsher, but ones I have been lucky

What the Yanks were up to. All-alloy 500 engine with open US TT-style pipes – and twin-carb option for 1957. The 650 had to have it!

1957 T100's optional alloy HDA 'Delta' cylinder head, with splayed exhaust and inlet ports, built up demand for a twin carb 650.

Rear-set controls on this T100 were part of the Race Kit.

enough to sample seemed remarkably smooth. It must be a question of "Compared to what?" The pre-unit set-up did absorb the shakes better than what would follow, and magneto ignition/dynamo lighting machines could retain the effective Triumph crankshaft shock absorber, which the alternator that had been adopted for economy by the touring models lost, in favour of one incorporated in the clutch. And at this point Turner was still keeping production relatively low at around 20,000 machines a year, meaning that Meriden's 1800 workforce were turning out a well-built product, as low warranty claims confirmed.

Triumph's twin-cylinder engine did have a lot going for it. Its twin gear-driven camshafts, positioned fore and aft of the cylinder, meant that by varying the camshaft mix it could be infinitely versatile, succeeding as anything from a 350 trials iron to a 650 roadburner. The hemispherical cylinder head with valves set at 90 degrees was a sound design, though the deep chambers and wide valve angles were ultimately limiting factors. And the front pushrod cover tube did obscure airflow to the engine, and particularly the air flow over the cylinder head. A cooler-running alloy head was therefore potentially a particular advantage.

Triumphs suffered a number of well-known weak spots. The engines leaked oil: the gearbox, the joints of the two separate bolted-on rocker boxes, and famously, the pushrod tubes, were some of the prime candidates. The exhaust camshafts wore rapidly, despite ongoing factory efforts. The engine's double-plunger oil pump, which had its circulation increased for the T110, lacked efficient oil filtration and was a design vulnerable to dirt; this could score the pump's bores, cause non-return valves to fail to seat, and eventually stop the pump working. A Morgo replacement pump was a favoured Rocker choice.

The 650 Triumph engine for 1954's T110 had been redesigned with a stiffened-up 3-piece crankshaft, with increased shaft diameters, and con rods of increased

Left: Non-standard rear units with exposed springs were popular in the US, but would not be adopted in UK for another decade. Plates for race numbers were part of the kit.

section, with their plain white metal bearings. The timing side ball-race main bearing was enlarged to duplicate the one on the drive side. This "big bearing" motor was signified by a small crescent-shaped bulge on the redesigned timing cover, and provided a safe basis for further tuning. The cylinder head, while still held down by 8 studs and still in iron, was redesigned with modified ports and larger inlet valves, as well as different finning. For 1954 only it was fitted with a

1956 T110 with new alloy cylinder head. Note "big bearing" bulge on primary chaincase, and stylish but fracture-prone two-level seat.

1956 Tiger's 8inch sls front brake retained previous ventilating air-scoops, but lacked 1954's "crinkle hub". Alloy wheel rims were a frequently fitted aftermarket goodie to "add lightness".

1957 T110, seen here with optional blue lower tank with cream tank top and mudguards paint finish, and that year's new "mouth-organ" tank badges.

650 c.c. TWINS

TIGER 110

The Triumph name has always been associated with performance, but in the 650 c.c. "Tiger 110" performance capabilities are available which exceed those of any standard production type motorcycle. Despite its high power output the engine is smooth-running, tractable and easy to start. It has an alloy cylinder head of advanced design, high compression pistons, special camshafts and a large bore carburetter. First class suspension, really powerful brakes and exceptional ease of control all combine to make the T110 a motorcycle of rare quality. The photograph illustrates the two-tone (Ivory/Blue) finish available as an optional extra on the T110 and T100.

regular 1⅛-inch Amal Type 29X carburettor, but with a TT-pattern float chamber. After that year, it adopted Amal's Monobloc. The '54, despite its iron head, would go on to develop a reputation as the fastest T110.

The new cycle parts to suit the new frame included a smarter stepped twinseat, black with white piping (though over time the seat pan on these invariably fractured where the front and rear portions joined.) The mid-section was tidied up with a "Streamstyle" unit incorporating toolbox, air-cleaner, battery and an oil tank catalogued at 6 pints but in reality only holding 5. Silencers on the characteristic Triumph 1¾-inch big bore exhaust pipes became a

THE TRIUMPH "SLICKSHIFT" GEARCHANGE

All Triumph 500 c.c. and 650 c.c. twins are now fitted with automatic clutch operation. Movement of the gearchange pedal releases the clutch and enables gearchanging to be carried out with this one action only. The handlebar clutch lever is retained and over-rides the auto mechanism if used. Quicker, easier gearchanging results from this interesting new development.

1958-on "Slickshift" provided automatic clutch action, but was never popular and most were disconnected.

"tear-drop" style, tapering at the rear and with a wonderfully throaty note. The front brake was a new single-sided 8-inch one with an air-scoop and an attractively scalloped, wavy spoke flange – for that year only, as it proved prone to fracture. The brakes on test worked well (29½ft stop from 30mph). Finish was the brilliant Shell Blue Sheen on the 4-gallon tank, the mudguards and the lined wheel centres, with black for everything else.

There were some teething troubles. Hughie Hancox related how machines were returned with fractured rear frame stays. They were brazed onto the castings taking the mounting plates for the silencers and footrest assemblies. Probably movement of the silencers had stressed the brazing; certainly the frame tubes were cracking immediately above the brazed lug. A stiffening brace, to reduce silencer movement, cured this. More seriously, the T110 engine with its increased compression (8.5:1 for export to the US with its higher octane fuel) proved prone to hot running, with the iron cylinder head on long fast runs overheating, distorting and warping, leading to blown head gaskets. Loss of power could also be caused by poor carburation from the common problem of rocker box caps unscrewing and detaching themselves due to vibration. The 8-stud head was also prone to

cracking between the valve seat edge and the studs, though often enough the cracks caused no problem.

The elephant in the room, however, was Triumph high-speed handling. That this was a problem was undisputed, and well-recognised at the time – by the late Fifties, when I took to two wheels, even I knew that "Triumphs don't handle." And it could be a lethal flaw. T110 rider Fred Johnson told Duckworth, "Sometimes it seemed like someone was getting killed every week," and Triumphs' weave and whip had to take its share of responsibility for that, as power outputs rose. The principle reason was that the new chassis's swinging-arm was unbraced to the frame, which turned the seat pillar it was attached to into a torsion bar as cornering pressures pushed the frame out of shape. Café racer Mike Clay wrote, "When pushed hard…any [pre-unit] 650 Triumph went round corners like a three-legged camel. In the cafés there was never any serious argument about the Triumph frame, no matter what the magazine road testers tried to tell us." The seasoned and quick journalist Dave Minton confirmed that "If you ever want to frighten yourself, give an early swinging-fork [Triumph] 650 lash round a mountain road."

Osborne in 1954 had praised the T110's handling as "good" – and compared to previous or contemporary plunger-sprung machinery, and definitely to Triumph's former Spring Hub, it probably was. Also he was a mature, experienced rider, and the test bike was brand new. Triumph's swinging-arm rear fork spindle required regular, frequent lubrication via an inaccessible grease nipple. If this was neglected the fork arm bushes and spindle wore badly, and the

handling seriously suffered. I've experienced this on two Triumphs, and it was frightening.

The other qualifier is that, as Triumph's popularity indicated, the handling could be lived with. It was OK if edgy at normal speeds, and the high-speed work, if the bike was well fettled, involved predictable behaviour whose limits could be learned, along with techniques to take you to the edge of those limits. Rocker Jerry Clayton, for instance, used advice from a John Surtees book on how drift could be countered by moving body weight to the inside of the bike to keep it as upright as possible. In general, you powered through corners and never throttled back once committed.

For years, though I realised that I was no speed merchant, it used to puzzle me why anyone would buy something which in such a vital area performed worse than the opposition, and terrified you while doing so. Then my classic bike journalism one day got me a ride on a Norton P11, one of the AMC hybrid twins with the exhilarating 750 Atlas engine shoe-horned into a lightweight Matchless frame. I found myself roaring at speed up a long country hill, with the motor on a rising throttle and the chassis squirming perceptibly beneath me, both I and the bike feeling barely in control but exhilaratingly alive, riding the crest of a wave of disaster at what the photographer driving behind confirmed was 90mph-plus. I finally understood that the sensation of being on the edge with a bike, but just not quite over it, could have a unique appeal. "We all loved Triumphs, they were quick," said Rocker and specials builder Bob Innes. "That's why we all bought them."

1958 T110 with black and Ivory two-tone colour scheme, unpopular as it resembled Police bikes too closely.

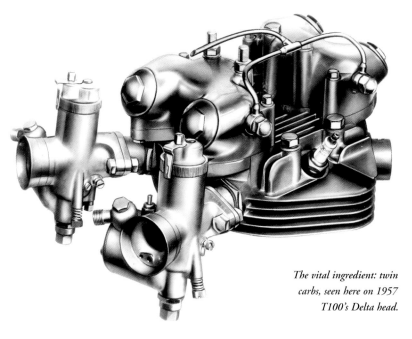

The vital ingredient: twin carbs, seen here on 1957 T100's Delta head.

Triumph 650 twin engine layout.

In the light of the overheating problems, the T110 for 1955 had an extra cooling fin on the cylinder head, which remained iron but was painted silver to look like alloy, a move which provoked mirth in the cafés. And a minor effort was made to address another element of the Triumph's poor handling, the slim telescopic front forks with their "inside springs", which gave 6½ inches of movement but featured long stanchions prone to bending under stress, and "minimum of metal" yokes which lacked lateral support, plus a long, under-braced steering head downtube. For 1955 the fork stem was made a little stiffer by fitting larger clamp bolts in the lower fork crown.

1956 saw a more serious attempt to tackle the T110's overheating (which Bob Innes believed often stemmed from impatient riders failing to let their motors warm up properly). There was a new die-cast light alloy cylinder head, with cast-in air passages. Because of its splayed-exhaust's shape when seen from above, it was known as the Delta head. Instead of each valve lying in a separate chamber in the head, there was now a chamber each for the pair of inlet and the pair of exhaust valves, with valve inserts of austenitic iron. The previous external oil lines were deleted, with oil now draining down pushrod tubes which had been redesigned, as had the rocker boxes. Despite still proving prone to crack, the head did run cooler, and standard compression was now 8.5:1. The con rods had also been strengthened, and revised to take shell bearings. Steady 90mph running now became a reality, with top speed reaching 110mph.

1956 also saw the introduction of the dual-purpose TR6 Trophy, predominantly for US export, which as it became to "single-carb Bonnie" spec would a) influence the T120's style, and b) be the favourite 650 of those who should have known, Meriden's own road testers. It would not be until mid-1962 that the 650 Trophy would be offered for the Home and General Export market as a dedicated roadster, the TR6SS, though it would always live in the shadow of the glamorous twin-carb Bonneville.

For 1957 the home market T110's compression reverted to 8.0:1, but the "mouth-organ" tank badges and optional two-tone paint schemes distracted from this; the standard colour changed to the attractive Silver Grey. The T110 got a new front brake, still single-sided. 1958 took a step backward in the style department, with a black-over-white UK colour option being too like the cops; new deeper valanced mudguards front and rear, when the boys wanted blades, preferably in alloy; and a full-width, cast-iron hub 8-inch single leading shoe front brake, matched by a similar cable-operated 7-inch one at the rear, neither of which looked or performed as well as before.

1957 T110, elegant in Silver Grey standard finish.

On the hooligan side, the exhaust pipes, now down to 1½-inch diameter, were given a very slight upward bend, and ran into silencers which for that year only were unbaffled. Claimed bhp rose to 42. The Delta head was modified to beat the cracks, with the combustion sphere reduced in size, together with reshaped piston crowns, plus inlet and exhaust valves with smaller diameter heads to suit. This left more metal between the valve seat and the nearest holding-down stud. These engines didn't go quite as well, but well enough, as this was the year that Hailwood and Shorey broke the Gold Star's grip and won the Thruxton 500 outright. And sensationally the 650 Tiger 110 now offered the option of the same twin-carb kit as the 500 had the previous year. This consisted of a pair of 376 Monoblocs mounted on splayed inlets via screwed-in steel adaptors, locked with large nuts and with short bell-mouth intakes.

The clamour for this, particularly in the States, became irresistible, even to the cautious Edward Turner, now 57 years old and suffering from diabetes. His contract specified that he spend half the year in America, which he found congenial and where, more than others, he had opened up the market for British motorcycles. He knew the Yankee appetite for sporting machinery and made a point of attending enduros like the Big Bear Run, where 650 Triumphs were dominant.

It was at this American sports segment that the new big twin-carb roadster was predominantly aimed. Turner's vision for the UK and European centred on the smaller-capacity, cheaper to produce C-range, with its unit construction, alternator electrics, and rear panels which with their cheerful paint and concealed mechanicals sought to tap into the all-conquering appeal of scooters. This turned out to be a blind alley, as well as a non-starter in America and of no interest to the café crowd.

So the sports 650 experienced a second coming in 1959 as the T120, which would make the T110 yesterday's man. Its twin-carb option was abruptly withdrawn for 1959, and the baffles went back in the silencers. 1960 brought "bath-tub" rear panelling adapted for the 650 B-range, and its accompanying florid front mudguard, for the T110; and though its magneto remained, the dynamo was replaced by an alternator. 1961 was the last year, with the TR6SS set to take over as the sports cruiser. How were the mighty fallen.

TECHNICAL SPECIFICATIONS: 1954 TRIUMPH T110

Capacity	649cc
Bore	71mm
Stroke	82mm
Compression	8.0:1
Power output	40bhp@6500rpm
Electrical system	6 volt
Ignition	Magneto
Generator	Dynamo
Wheels and tyres	F: 3.25x19. R: 3.50x19
Brakes	F: 8-inch. R:7-inch
Weight (dry)	395lbs
Max speed	114mph

"100mph standing still" – that was the slim, eager 1961 T120 Bonnie.

T120 BONNEVILLE

"In my youth...making personal statements via your choice of transport was easy, it was either Triumph or Norton...I well remember the scorn with which I viewed the Norton rider whilst aboard my Duck Egg blue and orange Bonnie. It was a matter of personal honour that no Norton ever out-accelerated you or in fact, ever passed you under any circumstances. The fact that I managed to survive the mid-Sixties obviously reflects the wimpish nature of most Norton owners of the time, because the single downtube-framed Bonnie was possibly the worst-handling bike ever built..."

Motorcycle journalist Rick Kemp

Turner appeared to be uncertain about releasing the T120 right until the last minute, so much so that when the decision was taken it was already too late to include it in the introductory catalogue for 1959. Throughout 1958 testing had been continuous on a prototype T110 with a strengthened engine and twin carbs. Despite the way the charismatic name, nodding at the '56 World Speed Record, would eclipse all others over the next 30 years and more, originally, as Hughie Hancox put it, "the Bonneville was a natural derivative of the twin carb T110."

The strengthening involved a new forged one-piece crankshaft in EN 16B steel, with larger, 1⅛-inch journals. A central 2¼-inch wide cast iron flywheel was threaded over the outer crank cheek, pressed into place and then secured, like the revised one on BSA's 1958 A-range, by three radial bolts passing through the outer rim of the flywheel into threaded holes in the crankshaft itself; the bolts were modified in midyear. Big end shells were retained for the stronger H-section alloy con rods. The bobweights' crank cheeks were straight-sided, and the 650's balance factor was 50%. The T120's 8.5:1 c.r. pistons had progressively thicker crowns, and their skirts were

modified to clear the new bobweights.

The T120's most visibly striking difference was of course its twin carbs. The set-up on its own offered little extra performance. What the twin carbs did allow, as the Americans had discovered, was wilder valve timing, which really did mean superior cylinder filling and gas flow, largely benefitting the top end of performance. With hot camshafts keeping the valves open longer, and an optional three-keyway valve-timing facility (standardised during 1962) allowing the rider to time the engine accordingly, every bit of power could be wrung from the top end. And in addi-tion, twin carbs to an onlooker shouted "Speed!" Their downside was increased thirst, and the continual need to keep them in balance. Hancox was not alone in thinking that "for the ordinary bloke the benefit was nil." But for the speed-mad Rockers it was a price they were willing to pay.

For the T120's inception the carburettor set-up was uncompromising. It consisted of a pair of 1¹⁄₁₆-inch Monoblocs on the Delta head, with the splayed, screw-in inlet ports on flanged steel mounting stubs, secured by large nuts. The carbs themselves featured no choke and no tickler buttons. They were

1961 T120, when everything had come good.

The first 1959 T120 Bonneville, the "Tangerine Dream" in all its glory.

"chopped", with their float bowls removed. In place was a single remote float bowl from Amal's GP instrument. This was suspended from the seat tube and rubber mounted. The set-up gave a real advantage at the top end, with a 1961 road test finding available revs rising from 6800 to 7500. But hard braking or acceleration caused surging in the float bowl and misfiring. This continued despite a mid-season kit with a metal extension plate to move the bowl three inches forward.

The T120 was race-oriented in an impractical way,

but that didn't stop it being an instant sensation as it arrived for 1959, the peak year for motorcycling in the UK. The new "super-sportster" also had remarkably little opposition then and for the next two years. AJS/Matchless twins had only expanded to the desirable full 650 capacity for 1959 and would experience crankshaft-breaking and tank-splitting teething troubles, while Norton twins only reached the 650 capacity in the UK for 1962. Meanwhile there was only Royal Enfield's flawed Constellation, and the sports BSA A10 Super Rocket, which a) was lumbered with a headlamp cowling plus heavy (and heavy-looking) cycle parts, and b) at 43bhp against the T120's 46bhp, the BSA was marginally down on power and speed at the top end. Plenty of Rockers opted for the sports A10's all-rounder durability and better handling, but there was no doubt which was the Daddy in the speed and charisma stakes. From 1959 till 1962, Triumphs ruled.

The familiar Triumph scarcity added to the initial appetite for them in the UK, as the majority of these first Tangerine and Pearl Grey T120s went to the USA. There, two things worked against them. The eye-catching colour scheme proved a rare Turner misjudgement in that department. The Yanks hated it, and in fact T120s produced in the second part of the year were painted Pearl Grey and Royal Blue (Azure, in America), the following model year's finish. Reaction to the "Tangerine Dream" in the UK was mixed; for Ace habitué Bob Innes "it was I think one of the best colours."

But even UK voices agreed that the overall styling, carried over from 1958's T110, failed to suit or to convey the new model's sporting nature. "Beautiful as it was," wrote Hughie Hancox, "it was old hat." The nacelle with its "Rev-u-lator" speedo and fork shrouds, the big petrol tank, the touring seat, the valanced mudguards, were all execrated Stateside, where, frustratingly, the single-carb dual-purpose TR6 was already being offered with the style they liked – separate chromed headlamp shell (which also allowed a wider choice of handlebar), 3 Imp. gallon gas tank, fork gaiters and sports mudguards. Piles of Tangerine Dream bikes accumulated in US warehouses, as riders instead ordered TR6s with a pricey twin-carb conversion. The following model year, T120s were re-categorised in the States as the TR7A/TR7B for that year only, just to distance them from the 1959 T120.

Meriden heeded this, as well as the groundswell of discontent about the way the T120's additional power highlighted the weaknesses of Triumph's frame and forks. "When the Bonnie came out in 1959," said Bob Innes, "that was a diabolical thing for handling.

King of the Road. 1961 Bonnie was the bike to have, and you can see why.

Fast mover. 1961 T120 was where it all came together – looks, speed, and a bit better handling.

Looking back, it's amazing anyone survived, they were bendy old things." And in the factory at ground level, Ariel expert Jim Lee, then a Meriden road tester, wrote of "some initial concern…as a result of [the Bonneville] not being much improved in terms of speed to that of [the T110]. I well remember the *Motor Cycling* magazine copy of the 1954 road test where a Tiger 110 had exceeded 115mph through the lights at MIRA. Someone had used a marker pen to write beneath that road test, 'What Happened?'" But Jim added that "under the guidance of [Frank Baker's] Experimental department the Bonneville was quickly 'speeded up'."

So after a less than fairy-tale debut, for 1960 the Bonneville appeared substantially re-styled, with a brand new twin-downtube frame and new forks. The frame was still of brazed-lug construction, though the bolted-on rear sub-frame featured new welded-on loops, replacing the previous silencer/footrest support. The top rail remained a single one, so the petrol tank rested on a pair of brazed-on mounting brackets attached to the downtubes (a design which possibly stressed the downtubes). The tank itself was fastened by a Norton-style broad metal top strap.

The redesigned front forks featured stiffer springs and a greater volume of oil for the damping, which was now claimed to be two-way. Their sliders carried bosses to take a strip middle-bridge for the front

mudguard. The suspension, thus stiffened up, gave less comfort but better handling. The rear units too would gain stiffer springs for 1962. With a new fork crown, and the steering head angle changed from 64.5 to 67 degrees (it would change again to a US/UK compromise of 65 degrees for 1961), while the riding position became a little more "jockey-like", the frame's handling was judged a real reassuring improvement.

The engine was altered so that although the magneto for ignition remained, secondary electrics were now handled by a crankshaft-mounted alternator. Adapting the crankcases meant that the new

All the good things – twin carbs, alloy head, magneto.

Modest side-cover transfer. Triumph let the splayed carbs speak for themselves

frame would only take the new engine. In the gearbox, the ratios were slightly lowered to cater for the US fixation on standing-quarter times, so acceleration became truly explosive for its time, with 0-60 in 6.5 seconds. The carburettor layout was first adjusted, with the float chamber now vertically suspended from the engine head-steady. But in the light of persisting fuel surge problems, in mid-1960 the set-up altered to two complete Monoblocs, each with a float chamber. Still hesitation and stalling at low speed remained, until later in the model year the two inlet manifolds were linked by a balance tube, which cured it.

And the Bonnie now looked as fast as it went, since it adopted the TR6's chromed headlamp shell, which permitted the fitting of clip-ons, and of the optional rev counter beside the separate new Chronometric speedo. There were gaiters for the forks; the 3-gallon tank as an original equipment option for all markets; a new, better-padded but slimmer seat; and a painted alloy blade front mudguard, matched by an unvalanced steel rear one. The headlamp was QD to simplify removal for competition, but its connector plug developed a reputation for spontaneously disconnecting, usually at night. Overall, however, the makeover was a truly effective transformation, with

By 1961, more sporting gaiters had replaced the original T120's metal shrouds for the slim front forks.

Triumph surfing the Zeitgeist once more. The best finish came for 1961, with the mercurial combination of Sky Blue and Silver Sheen. The effect was of something simultaneously powerful yet almost feminine in its slim, eager lightness. "They were very dainty, really," said one Triumph man " – but all us butch berks wanted one!"

And no wonder. A *Motor Cycling* test published in June 1961 found a consistent 108mph top speed on a standard T120R, with 43mph achievable in first, 62 in second, and 87 in third. But the testers emphasised that this impressive performance had not been achieved with any loss of flexibility or tractability ("In London traffic it was one of the most pleasant machines we have ever used"), with a range of acceleration in fourth from 30mph all the way to above 100, and no power band to seek out. The plot ticked over reliably, started easily hot or cold (ticklers were in place but still no choke), the ride was comfortable, and 64mpg was returned overall. All this had been achieved primarily by the intelligent choice of the hot E3134 camshaft for the inlet and the slightly milder E3325 for the exhaust, with everything else tuned to suit.

There was more. The magazine then carried out a supplementary test at MIRA, headlining it "The Fastest Production Roadster", after simply reinstalling the previous remote float chamber carburettor set-up – everything else, they said, was standard, bar racing tyres and a 4.00 x 18 rear wheel (which would be offered as an option the following season). 7500rpm was now attainable, meaning 50 mph in first, 70 in second, 92 in third and a mean top speed of 116.9mph in fourth. This was the tool,

' 61 Bonnie looked like a fast, eager lady – and appearances were not deceptive.

Bonneville spirit, a combination of great looks and blistering performance, though never at the expense of tractability.

they concluded, if you wanted "a 650 that really does march."

Downsides from the regular test were the brakes (35ft stopping from 30mph), despite the floating shoes introduced for 1961; the lights; and the shakes – "vibration was not absent," they delicately stated, adding hastily "but was never excessive. There were no periods..." As well as the loss of the excellent engine-shaft shock absorber when the alternator had been adopted, T120 vibration had in fact increased as a result of an unfortunate discovery back in the 1960 model year.

TECHNICAL SPECIFICATIONS:
1961 TRIUMPH T120R BONNEVILLE

Capacity	649cc
Bore	71mm
Stroke	82mm
Compression	8.5:1
Power output	46bhp@6500rpm
Electrical system	6 volt
Ignition	Magneto
Generator	Alternator
Wheels and tyres	F: 3.25x19. R: 3.50x19
Brakes	F: 8-inch. R: 7-inch
Weight (dry)	390lbs
Max speed	108.2mph

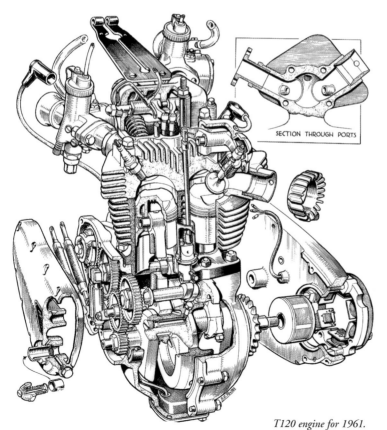

SECTION THROUGH PORTS

T120 engine for 1961.

At the Big Bear Run enduro in Dec 1959 Edward Turner had witnessed a Triumph rider thrown off and killed when his 650's frame fractured below the headstock. Immediate prolonged factory testing at MIRA led to the frame's design being altered in mid-1960 to include a lower tank rail, which could be retro-fitted, to brace the steering head. This was successful, but it increased vibration. One of the common side-effects was fracturing of the petrol tank's centre fixing band, aggravated by owners over-tightening them. This was only cured after five variations in the strap's material, when they finally settled in mid-1962 on stainless steel.

Mute recognition of the problem of shakes, common to all sports parallel twins, also came in 1961 with a strengthened petrol tank nose, and rubber mounting for the toolbox, followed for 1962 by the same for the oil tank. More fundamentally, for the pre-units' final 1962 season, changes came for the crankshaft, with pear-shaped webs and a slightly wider flywheel giving progressively higher balance factors, until a permanent 85% was settled on. 1962's new, heavier crank did damp down some vibration, and if it took a little off throttle response, it also, for the US, gave improved torque and bite for the rear wheel in the dirt.

Another difficulty was also tackled in the electrical department, where there had been overcharging problems leading to boiled batteries and spilled acid, due to the alternator output being poorly matched to the magneto ignition. After interim wiring solutions and then a new harness, 1962's adoption of a Lucas RM19 alternator with a low output stator, plus a new rectifier, solved the problem – just before the coming of the unit Bonnie with its all-alternator electrics, and a whole new world of grief… Meanwhile in mid-1962 the troublesome QD headlamp was retired.

The Bonneville was flying high, as emphasised by John Holder/Tony Godfrey's overall win at Thruxton for 1961. For the cowboys, nothing would ever come up to it. Fast enough as standard, though from that year just being aced by the 650 Norton opposition, Triumphs had the benefit of everything from the factory TIB tuning bulletins, to the lads' own efforts such as lightening flywheels, plus after-market go-faster options like Dunstall swept-back exhausts and "Decibel" silencers, ARE alloy barrels, twin-plug heads and Morgo big bore conversions. The scene might fade, and the pre-units which had exemplified it might pass in favour of better-handling if harsher unit successors. But for die-hards, nothing would touch the legendary pre-unit T120 Bonneville.

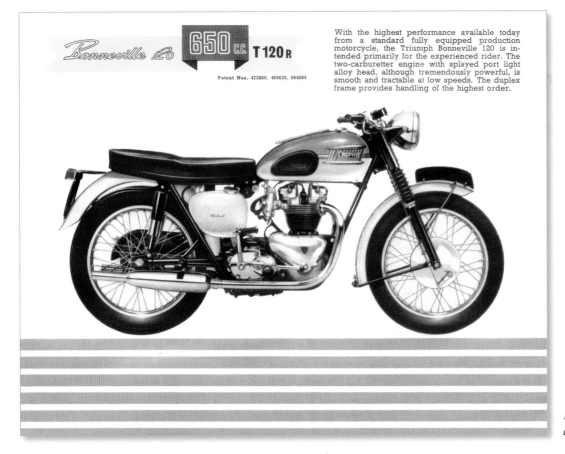

1962 T120R, swansong for the pre-unit Bonneville.

CHAPTER 5:
ROYAL ENFIELD 700 CONSTELLATION

It was an iconic image taken early in 1963 at night from a low angle, a Royal Enfield big twin thundering fast by the camera, rider's scarf streaming, next to a banner headline screaming: SUICIDE CLUB! On the front page of the **Daily Mirror***'s shock-horror anti-Rocker edition.*

1958 Constellation ridden at speed past the Ace Café on the A406 North Circular road, in February 1961. This article caused a crackdown on ton-up boys. Enfield twins always were unlucky!

Big – the biggest! Brash, fast, powerful and powerful-looking, covered in chrome – how could Enfield's Constellation twin possibly miss?

But by then, it already had…

R oyal Enfield were singular in all sorts of ways. The company was located 15 miles south of the Birmingham/Coventry nexus in the Worcestershire town of Redditch, where they occupied a substantial 37-acre site employing a workforce of up to 1500. The company produced 15,000 bicycles a year; stationary engines including a corrosion-proof diesel; military predictor equipment and even instruments for the Atomic Energy Authority, emphasising their reputation for precision engineering. They were proud of the fact that most operations could be carried out in-house. Many progressive features could be found on their motorbikes, often originating with them, such as the "cush-hub" rear wheel transmission shock absorber, as well as the early adoption of swinging-arm suspension, especially prominent on their successful off-road Bullet singles.

Yet their motorcycle output remained relatively small. No more than 2000 were built of the machine under consideration, the mighty 700 Constellation, over a six-year production run. In this as in their design and jumbo engine size, the big Enfield twins, as author Mike Clay put it, "had a character all of their own."

The company Chairman and MD was ex-RFC pilot Major Frank Walker Smith, a son of the original founder. Major Smith ran the show, and some have felt that his reluctance to plan for high volume production, to speculate by investing in bulk raw materials and new plant (though Enfield was better than some in the latter respect), fatally limited the company. Yet it was a pleasant place to work (just as well, since wages were notably low), but even that

could be a drawback. Blunt Yorkshire Royal Enfield agent Wilf Green wrote, "I was dismayed by the lack of drive emanating from Enfield…the pleasant family "caring" attitude… was not acceptable for success in the post-war marketing and production climate…"

Major Smith's chief designer was Ted Pardoe, and the head of production development since 1925 had been Tony Wilson-Jones, a theoretically-minded boffin who often contributed papers to the Institute of Mechanical Engineers: "If you asked him the time he'd tell you how a watch worked," one colleague recalled. A distinctive, substantial, 16-stone figure who rode a little Royal Enfield 125 – "when he wore his big gabardine motorcycle coat and waders, you had a job to see the motorcycle" – Wilson-Jones, who had competed in trials pre-war, was more approachable than Major Smith, but with his pure engineering interests, perhaps not the best man to be in charge of product development.

Still, Royal Enfield had kept up well with post-war trends, Wilson-Jones designing two-way damped telescopic front forks for the range in 1946, and Ted Pardoe a 500cc parallel twin for 1949. In a "modular" tradition that would be followed on the 700, in essence the engine on this had been a doubled-up pre-war Model S 250, emphasised by the

twin's separate cylinder barrels and heads. This 25bhp motor was then slotted into the controversial swinging-arm cycle parts of the sporting dual-purpose Bullet single – controversial because most other off-roaders relied on a rigid rear end for optimum continuous rear wheel grip. The 500 twin (it never got a name) should have changed minds about that when collecting Golds and the Manufacturers awards in the tough 1951 ISDT. Until 1954, only AJS/Matchless and later Norton offered full swinging-arm suspension on their production motorcycles. Yet just 9000 of the successful Bullets would be produced in 13 years!

Contradictions abounded when the twin was

Compact, muscular and with lashings of chrome, the Constellation, here seen in 1960 guise, certainly had presence.

Close relative, a 500 Twin from 1952.

Ridden hard, and it's gone down hard a time or two – wonderfully unrestored 1961 Constellation. Given the crucial role Production racing played in the Constellation saga, this authentic, mechanically sound survivor may be quite a contrast with the examples from other marques, but with its rough edges and genuine factory racing accessories, it's survived to earn its place here, as a living example of how the need for speed over-rode cosmetic considerations back in the day.

expanded for 1953 to 692cc. Royal Enfield, innovative as ever, had leap-frogged the Triumph and BSA big boys to create what would be Britain's biggest twin after the Vincent had expired in 1955. They had done so by once again doubling-up, in this case taking the excellent 350 Bullet as the basis for the

separate cylinders, with the same 70 x 90mm dimensions. The latter arrangement, as also practiced by AJS/Matchless twins, had the benefits over a single solid cylinder block of good cooling and accessibility, plus half-price repairs in the event of a seizure or scoring on one barrel only. The downside in the case of the big Enfield was a loss of stiffness, which, as we shall see, would have unfortunate consequences, and contribute to the marque's (justified) nickname of "Royal Oilfield".

The contradiction came from the fact that having created the biggest parallel twin, the company offered it in a notably soft-tuned state (36bhp at 6000rpm, only 2bhp more than Triumph's cooking 6T650Thunderbird). It was common, and prudent, practice among manufacturers to put out a touring version of a model, only later followed by a sportier one, but this went on for three years; the gentle giant was clearly aimed at the sidecar market, which in the UK then accounted for one in three large-capacity motorcycles. At least they gave it a space age name, Meteor, and finished it distinctively in pleasant polychromatic Copper Beech. But none of that exactly set the pulses racing, either among the leather boys,

A suitable point of origin for this racerised 700 Royal Enfield.

or on the American market where Royal Enfields, marketed as Indians from 1955 to 1959, had a small but enthusiastic following. The Americanised Meteor, with high bars, separate headlamp, and a small tank, went out as the Indian Trailblazer.

It was reportedly in response to American demands that a rather more sporting version, the Super Meteor, appeared for 1956, putting out 40bhp at 5500rpm, and providing a better platform for the machine's development potential. There were bigger inlet valves, a stronger crankshaft with outer webs cut away, the pushrods altered, gearing raised, and both the iron barrels and alloy heads more heavily finned. The latter's head-locating spigot was deleted, replaced by two hollow dowels around the outer fixings and a revised head gasket. An alternator and magneto replaced the previous Magdyno. The speed of the oil pump was doubled by the fitting of a two-start worm to the typically Enfield twin

Royal Enfield's unique engine layout, showing filler cap for crankcase oil compartment, and behind kickstart, the patented neutral-finder lever on Albion gearbox.

oscillating-plunger oil pumps (at a time when most other manufacturers had gone to gear-type pumps). Good for 101mph, the Super Meteor was to be the basis of the truly sporting Constellation; although many of its features already contained the seeds of trouble.

"When are you going to do it up?" "Come off it, it's took me years to get it like this..."

Casquette was sawn off in the Sixties to allow fitting of twinned instruments and clip-ons. Top yoke is off an Enfield 250 Continental GT. Distressed custom paintwork reveals excellent quality of original chrome.

THE WORKS: THE 692CC ENGINE & GEARBOX

The Royal Enfield big twin featured a one-piece crankshaft with a central flywheel assembly and small outer flywheels. The two similar-sized main bearings which it ran on reversed the norm by using a single-row ball bearing on the more stressed drive side, and a roller on the timing side; but these were rarely trouble

Constellation's standard casquette, incorporating twin side-lights, 150 mph Smiths Chronometric speedo, ammeter, and alloy butterfly steering damper control.

spots. The crankcase castings were the same as those for the 500 twin. The primary chaincase cover was fastened by a single centre bolt, an excellent notion lifted by Norton for their Commando, and not normally a leak-point unless severely over-tightened. Behind it the primary chain was duplex, and tensioned by a slipper device.

Oil feed to the big ends was via the crankshaft. The crankpins were drilled out, and then sealed at either end with steel disks held in place by circlips, forming a reservoir for oil within, ensuring that there was never a dry start for the big ends. While the 500s had their big end caps secured by nuts and split pins, and as on the Bullets running directly on the shaft, the 700s fitted shell bearings and the big ends were retained by special socket-head cap screws.

As with the Bullet, the twin engine displayed a feature first found in a Royal Enfield in 1903, namely the 4 pints of engine oil being carried not in a conventional external tank but in a compartment in the base of the crankcase, behind the flywheel area. It also shared the same design of reciprocating oil pump as the singles, located in the one-piece timing cover, although the pumps differed in detail, and on the twin the cylindrical oil filter lay across the engine in a

Original spec 1960
Constellation, including
Armstrong rear dampers
and that year's mudguards,
before '61's semi-enclosure
at the rear.

Dual back-to-back 6 inch
front brakes looked well, but
were not always the most
efficient.

Twin splayed Monoblocs were adopted for 1960, with side-
panel "ears" to shield their intakes. Engine breathing
arrangements were also revised. Single-bolt primary chaincase
cover was often oil-tight, as here; Norton designers borrowed the
idea for the Commando.

Constellation debut for 1958.

covers, each fastened by four corner bolts, with the rockers running on spindles supported by the body of the casting. Valve springs were duplex and clearances tight, and the valves with hardened caps worked in pressed-in bronze guides. An inlet manifold was bolted to the rear faces of the heads, to carry a single carburettor.

The four-speed Albion gearbox, as on the Bullet, was bolted up to the rear of the crankcase. One reason was for compactness, and the big twin was remarkably so, retaining a 54-inch wheelbase to the end, while the Triumph equivalent was a couple of inches longer. (The exceptions were to be the later US variants, where the swinging-arm was lengthened by 3 inches to provide a rangier, bigger-looking bike, and perhaps also one better suited to desert riding.)

separate cast-in tunnel, not fore-and-aft as on the single. Almost all the oilways were internal. The engine breathed via the hollow drive-side mainshaft through a non-return disk valve to an external pipe.

Drive to the twin high-mounted fore-and-aft camshafts was by chain rather than by gear as on the singles, with a reversible quadrant plate to give maximum adjustment. The cylinder barrels were spigotted 3 inches deep into the crankcase. On top of the alloy cylinder head sat four distinctive humped rocker

Constellation for 1959.

The Albion gearbox was used for twins and singles. It featured the unique neutral finder, a small pedal mounted, inaccessibly for novices, inboard of the long gear pedal itself. It was operated by the rider's heel, from second, third, or fourth, to select neutral at a standstill, quite a handy facility at traffic lights, etc, though finding it from first would have been welcome. The Albion box internals featured only one selector fork, so that it moved all the gears at once. Despite the long pedal, the gearchange movement was short and required firm pressure and a follow-through to avoid false neutrals. The gears were very steeply cut back also, so that they stayed engaged, but could be reluctant to come apart, especially if the clutch was not functioning well. As journalist Peter Watson put it bluntly, "What a rotten thing to put on an otherwise sporting motorcycle."

This tall and chunky engine/gearbox, imposing to the point of menace to look at, formed a stressed member of the chassis, with its single top and down tubes. No machine is perfect, and the big twin worked well enough, with good mid-range acceleration, and was flexible and pleasant to ride if not thrashed. There had, however, been enough broken crankshafts to justify revision of the Super Meteor's larger journals. But occasional breakages continued, and the crank would be strengthened again for the Constellation.

The big twin engines were made not at Redditch but in another Royal Enfield facility, the five-storey Greenland Mills at Bradford-on-Avon (nearby lay the famous underground Westwood works, where twin production moved to in 1963, and where from 1966

the final 736cc Interceptor twins were to be made.) Roger Shuttleworth, in charge of the Mills' small experimental department, later confirmed that "the biggest problem was that the cylinder heads used to leak. I couldn't make a seal between the pushrod tubes in the cylinder head and the cylinder barrel. The main trouble was the different rates of expansion between the alloy cylinder head and the cast iron barrel. The rates of expansion of the two metals were so different that it was almost impossible to maintain a seal. I tried putting a little grommet round the top of the pushrod tube, and I also tried a compression ring round the top of the cylinder, but… I was never able to cure it 100%."

A more fundamental problem was that, with the separate cylinders, and the engine unit a stressed member of the less-than-stiff frame, the motor "shuffled" at the cylinder mouths, distorted, and could even work loose in the frame, with oil leaks, typically between the cylinders, severe vibration, and compromised handling from the flexing chassis, all resulting.

Another persistent problem was the fact that the engines ran hot, especially at speed, mainly because of the rapid heating of the minimal 4-pint oil supply – other twins had 5 or 6 pints – housed down in the engine room. When the big twins began to go production racing, purpose-built oil coolers were very soon offered, and later engines were drilled for them whether they were fitted or not. The oil pump too was always suspect; Enfield had retained the reciprocating design because they believed others had only adopted gear-type pumps to help stop wet-sumping, which was

Constellation in 1962. Note '61-on partial enclosure at rear.

Perhaps all Royal Enfield twins' real role was touring, as illustrated here on a 500.

not a problem for Redditch as its engine oil was there in the sump already! The twin oscillating-plunger pumps, unusually the same size for both feed and return functions, could cavitate at high speeds, interrupting the oil supply to the big ends. Royal Enfield experimented with different drive speeds and pump piston sizes, but troubles continued, including over-oiling of the bottom end.

One of the most intractable problems related to the lubrication, and that was the engine breathing. Riders learned to drill into the pressurised oil chamber and install a big breather pipe running back to the rear mudguard. Another useful move was replacing a rubber sleeve inside the timing side crankshaft with a tighter-fitting nylon substitute. This alone was said to double the oil pressure.

The Albion gearbox too could cause more than irritation when the 700s were driven hard. Luckily the big engine was so tractable that mostly you could get into top and stay there. But the box's design for the Constellation replaced a previous steel sleeve-gear with a gearbox shaft running in a sleeve of some length, originally bushed in bronze, with many holes drilled through the sleeve and bush, to lubricate the large plain bearing. But if the bush nipped up even slightly, as it might typically under hard initial acceleration, then it could turn in the

sleeve, closing up all the oilways. The transmission quality would deteriorate, the sleeve split, the shaft seize and the rear wheel lock up. When a customer was killed after this happened with his Constellation, Redditch tester Brian Crow circulated MIRA at full tilt (his fastest lap there on a Connie involved a maximum speed of 120.8mph) to try to recreate the accident. Which he did, with unhappy effects for his arms in the subsequent get-off…

But despite the horror stories (and there's more to come) let's remember that Syd Lawton, the man behind the Royal Enfield twins' frustrated and frustrating attempts to win at Production racing, called the 700 engine "a wonderful unit, strong and dependable, with the potential to be the best British vertical twin."

THE CONSTELLATION COMES

Although they often did not exploit their winners, Royal Enfield did have an ear to the ground, and were aware that by 1958 the spirit of motorcycling in the UK was changing. With teenage spending power growing, the average age of riders had dropped, and as the Rocker era moved into top gear, Triumph's "Ton-Ten" and BSA's 43bhp Super Rocket 650s were top dogs. And the US market too demanded as fast a roadburner as possible.

Bernal Osborne on the 1958 test run Constellation in Belgium, where a 115mph dash to the port raised interest in the new sports twin.

So for the UK in April 1958 Redditch once again leap-frogged the others, introducing the Constellation sportster with a claimed 51bhp at 6250rpm, which shortly after, on test with *Motor Cycling*, would top 115mph on Belgian highways. It looked the part too, with a massive, squareish 4½-gallon polychromatic burgundy and chrome petrol tank, chromed mudguards, a siamesed exhaust, a 150mph Smiths speedo and a big Amal TT9 carb. That chrome tank alone, one of the first to feature recessed knee-grips, was charisma personified; I can remember seeing one in a shop window and wanting to buy it, just to have it. The only downside for the café crowd was Enfield's headlamp casquette, adopted in 1954, which prohibited the fitting of dropped clip-on handlebars. The cowling also prevented twinned instruments being fitted, though a rev counter on a separate bracket was an optional extra – and the speedo in the Constellations casquette was a 150mph one – like a Vincent Black Shadow. This sat in front of another first for Enfield's solo big twins, a butterfly alloy steering damper knob.

The Constellation, which had been released previously for the US, saw some genuinely major revisions. For pragmatic reasons (the dies for the old crankcases were worn out), Enfield adopted a new crankcase for the new model and the other twins. This featured the same 70 x 90 mm dimensions as previously, but with the fore-and-aft camshafts now mounted even higher, by sinking the cylinders lower into the crankcase. The pushrods were shortened, as well as lightened by using alloy tubing for them, with induction-hardened steel ends. On the Connie the cams were of racing type without quietening ramps, with higher lift and longer opening dwell. Enfields featured user-friendly touches wherever possible, and these camshafts could be removed via the timing side, without splitting the cases.

Re-cast alloy cylinder heads also permitted opened-out inlet ports, plus Nimonic valves developed by Syd Lawton from BSA ones cut down to suit, and with Gold Star alloy caps and collets. The dual valve springs were based on American W and S ones. The exhaust valves were of EN54 austenitic steel with their stems Stellite-faced, and the inlet valves of EN52 silicone-chromium steel. These allowed higher revving in safety. The head and barrel finning was considerably increased again to combat the twins known problem of running hot at speed, which had contributed to the blown head gaskets. The crankshaft, already strong, was now in 40/45 ton/in² spheroidal graphite nodular iron, with bigger crankpin diameters of 1⅞ inch – dimensions Triumph twins would only reach in 1970! Compression was raised from the Super Meteor's 7.25:1 to 8.5:1, taking advantage of the

*Early 1961 Constellation, with
the new 3-part tail-fin silencer,
but not the revised seat and
rear enclosure.*

higher octane fuel now available. An attempt was made to diminish over-oiling of the bottom end by replacing the previous drive-side bearing's felt washer, located in the steel housing at the back of the chaincase behind the engine sprocket, with a neoprene oil seal.

After the first few Constellations, their engines were both statically and (expensively) also dynamically balanced – because vibration from the 692cc twin with its raised compression had proved unbearable at speed. The gearing had been lowered slightly in the interests of blinding acceleration. The balancing helped, but vibration above 80mph remained severe, and over 90mph it could knock your feet off the pegs. As Wilf Green, the plain-spoken Northern dealer put it, "The Constellation was one of the very few (true) ton-up models, a real galloper, but the balance factor was suspect as the vibration when really motoring was horrendous."

The Constellation retained an alternator, but for ignition, like the original Super Meteor, had a manually-controlled Lucas K2F magneto. Another main problem area as the twins' output had risen had been the clutch, so for the Connie, Tony Wilson-Jones had designed an all-new "scissors" clutch, so-called because its operating mechanism featured two levers, one fixed, one moving, which met at a pivot point like scissors. Unconventionally the mechanism (but not the clutch itself) was mounted in the primary case.

The 6-spring clutch was face-operated, with a shaft worked by a ball-and-ramp outboard of the clutch itself. This design quickly proved inadequate: fast riders on the street recalled how in traffic, unable to withstand any slipping, all its clearance disappeared, leaving them with no means of disconnecting the drive. On the track, Lawton's top rider at the benchmark Thruxton 500 production races, hard-charging Bob McIntyre, in 1959 led for a while on a Connie, but after experiencing bad clutch problems, crashed and was out. The factory would tacitly acknowledge the mechanism's failure by a complete redesign for 1961.

The big new twin did look sensational, however, with its imposingly tall front end created by a combination of the long forks, the frame design and the tank shape, bulked out at its front end. Even the casquette was aggressive, like a boxer's tucked in chin, while the massive engine/gearbox lump breathed power. There was enough chrome – Redditch had its own plating plant – to satisfy the need for flash, on mudguards, the tank, the rear chainguard and the siamesed exhaust with its cigar-shaped silencer. The latter feature was a victory of style over substance; in the 1958 Thruxton race Lawton had chosen to put his top rider McIntyre on a Super Meteor with its head modified like a Constellation, partly because the previous model ran twin exhausts, and Lawton considered that the siamesed system marginally cut acceleration.

Magnificent 1960 Constellation.

Another big piece of go-faster eye candy, the launch bike's TT9 1⅜-inch carburettor, was also of dubious value, as the TT flooded too easily, particularly if the bike was on its side stand, making for difficult hot starting. This was also caused by its absence of a throttle stop, so that the throttle cable stretched under the weight of the instrument's heavy slide, altering the starting characteristics. Syd Lawton had already told the company that a single 389 Monobloc suited the grunty engine best, but though one had been fitted for the latter half of the 1959 model year as the company backed away from the TT carb, for 1960 fashionable Bonneville-type twin Monoblocs were fitted – and hot-starting problems returned, due to fuel vaporising because the carbs were mounted too close to the hot cylinder head.

Looks aside, the Constellation's impressive top speed figures were the magnet, irrespective of how long the big twin could maintain them – *Motor Cycling's* bike in Belgium had ended up covered in oil, when during a last blast at the end of 1958's high-speed run (65 miles in 46 minutes, averaging 82.8 from a standing start), one of the rocker oil-feed pipes had come off at its union. But this was still the fastest standard production twin you could buy that year, the T110's 115mph having been achieved with the help of a factory breathed-on engine. On real roads the Connie could be a strong contender, with spectacular mid-range acceleration from 40-60, and exiting a

roundabout the 700 would blow off any Triumph. The mistake was to run up the revs in the gears. As then Club racer Ray Knight put it when he blew up his second one, "I had achieved 7000rpm too many times, a practice I learned was really pushing the old thing much too hard." On the street, speed could be taken from 40mph to 110in top gear. The brakes, twin back-to-back 6-inch front ones with their twin cables balanced by a handlebar-mounted beam or "whiffle tree compensator," needed careful and correct balancing, the right linings, and their floating cam spindles kept floating (i.e. not over-tightened), but in good condition, along with the 7-inch single leading shoe rear brake, could bring a 700 twin to a halt from 30mph in a competitive 29½ feet, although one owner called them "not quite as good as they look," and they lacked bite.

The handling had its minor quirks, including some pitching on fast bends, due to two factors. The first was uneven rebound damping from the Armstrong rear units with their two internal springs and knurled adjustor rings, which Enfield favoured after testing several units at MIRA. The second was the relative weakness of the long front forks with their leading spindle. One owner confirmed that standing astride the front wheel the bars could be wiggled well off-centre, even with the fork pinch bolts fully tightened; the heavy chrome mudguard doubled as a necessary fork brace. Syd Lawton would

Compact but beefy, the 1960 Constellation looked the business.

Period photo of 1961 Constellation shows details of siamesed exhaust.

stiffen them for racing by using Norton fork tubes. Ground clearance was limited on both sides by the awkward-to-use and insecure alloy centre stand, and for 1960 the factory tucked the exhaust/silencer joint in a little further. But the handling was never alarming and was compensated for by the grunt. As racer Ray Knight confirmed, ridden spiritedly "they were quite capable of holding their own with models from other manufacturers."

TROUBLE ON TWO WHEELS

As mentioned, since 1956 the big twins had been part of the burgeoning Production race scene, the cutting edge being the machines entered, with covert factory backing, by ex-Norton works rider Syd Lawton of Southampton dealers Lawton and Wilson. The works involvement seems to have been mostly one way – Lawton later wrote that "though I gave (the factory) a list of thirty different points that needed attention, very few of them were acted on – it was as if some people at the factory thought I was treading on their toes."

The principal event was fiercely contested by McIntyre, one very determined Scot, on the bumpy wartime airfield at Thruxton, and his efforts did initially have an effect. From 1958, both manufacturers and the public became heavily involved with this race, the latter because, as Mick Walker wrote, "A win at Thruxton was by now a major weapon for sales." Future TT racer and journalist Ray Knight in his book *Even More Speed* (Lily Publications) describes how his fast young crowd liked the Thruxton races for featuring "production machines, ones we were familiar with, unlike 'proper' racing machines in which we had little interest." In 1958, the year the endurance race changed from 9 hours to 500 miles, Ray wrote, "We witnessed the famous Bob McIntyre sweeping past works Triumphs on, of all things, a Royal Enfield Super Meteor." Bob Mac may have been sidelined that year with a split tank, so that Hailwood and Shorey's Triumph won, but Bob Mac/Derek Powell had finished just one lap behind Hailwood, Royal Enfields came second and third, twins had broken the previous grip of the Gold Star singles, and Ray was impressed enough to buy his first 700 Enfield for Club racing.

On the street, unfortunately, it was a different story. The vibration that had caused Bob Mac's split tanks in 1957 and '58, the all-too-evident oiling problems, the scissors clutch, the hot running ("burn-ups," wrote one Rocker, "could leave the oil compartment virtually empty"), and the continuing problem of the blowing head gaskets, with riders learning to listen for "a tell-tale cheeping noise – like a budgie", after which oil blew into the internal oilways and went everywhere – all this combined to convince the leather boys early on that the Constellation would not run hard and fast for long without problems.

A less frequent but more spectacular trouble was the way that in the primary chaincase, into which from 1960 the breathing system discharged, a spark from either the duplex primary chain running on its hardened steel slipper tensioner, or the RM15 alternator, could ignite the volatile gases and blow off the single-fixing primary chaincase cover! Finally, the relative scarcity of the model, plus a price of £295 when £10 less got you a T120 Bonneville, also didn't help.

1959's Constellation became known retrospectively as "the fast one" (the TT carb, higher compression), but on track that year McIntyre's early lead, clutch trouble and subsequent fall damaged its reputation fatally. 1960 saw Bob in contention again, this time with an experimental version of the conventional clutch which would replace the "scissors" type on the production line for 1961; but in the race, with a two-lap lead despite his co-rider having suffered a split exhaust bracket, the clutch began to fail in the third hour, then jammed the drive chain and locked the engine, flinging McIntyre off at speed. Finally in 1961 the clutch had been sorted for production, but according to Syd Lawton, Wilson-Jones fitted new "supposedly stronger" big-end bolts to the race engines, along with new con rods. Mac was leading from the start when a big-end bolt sheared at 115mph, though in the ensuing get-off mercifully he avoided major injury. After that Lawton successfully switched his efforts to the Norton twins.

OVER AND OUT

It must be said that the factory responded actively to the Connie's problems. 1960 saw a barrage of measures taken against the chronic vibration. The compression was dropped to 8.0:1; lighter pistons were used, with their bottom piston ring groove modified to contain two separate oil control rings. The cylinder head-steady became a torque stay from the head back to a lug now on the underside of the frame top tube. And the crankshaft's balance factor was increased from 50% to 75%, with the flywheels altered to bob-weights (Wilson-Jones believed a twin did not require as much flywheel weight as a single), with the crankshaft assembly's weight reduced by 4lbs to 24lbs.

Engine breathing was also overhauled, with a drive side flap valve now discharging through a special drilled bolt which screwed the alternator rotor to the end of its shaft. This bolt contained in its head a pen-steel disc, breathing into the primary chaincase. The

Hard man racer Bob McIntyre, frustrated three years running at Thruxton on the big Enfield.

Contemporary picture of 1961 Constellation's rear end with Armstrong dampers, though the manufacturer's name has been blanked out, BBC-style!

breather body on the chaincase replaced its previous plain neoprene pipe discharging to atmosphere, with a metal pipe leading oil via the oil compartment to the rear chain. And where the previous crankcase breather mechanism had been screwed onto the outside left of the crankcase, now a drainpipe conveyed excess oil from the camshaft tunnels and cylinder walls back to the oil compartment, with the drain connected to the annular cavities at the base of the cylinder. Wisely if a trifle ominously, a magnet to catch small debris was fitted to the main oil filter. These measures improved but did not cure the Constellation's breathing problems, and riders still found it wise to fit a large bore pipe to the top of the crankcase, leading to the rear mudguard and venting to atmosphere, to relieve pressure build-up in the crankcase.

The frame was changed from the rather heavy brazed original to a version of the all-welded one found for the '57-on Bullet. Twin Amal 376 Monobloc

Royal Enfield twin-cylinder engine layout, though this model featured coil and distributor electrics.

carburettors were also fitted that year, each mounted on a short, splayed inlet stub. The right-hand instrument had its float chamber cut and blanked off, being supplied from the left one by flexible piping linking the two main jet holders. The centre toolbox pressing was modified to include two "ears" at the front, to shroud the twin carburettors' intakes. The casquette was also altered, with its twin sidelights set further apart. In the light of those split tanks, the rear tank mounting was modified. And the friction plates in the clutch became Neolangite bonded.

The latter change was undercut the following year, as for 1961 a completely new, more conventional clutch was adopted, with a star-shaped outer plate and operated by a normal pushrod. The new clutch could still give problems, but now these would be due to faulty assembly or adjustment. The tank size was now catalogued at 4¼ gallons and its rear mounting was modified once more. The silencer became a new three-part "torpedo", still with no tail-pipe but carrying a polished cast-aluminium tail-piece with a narrow fin, and exhaust gases discharging downwards through a longitudinal slot in the underside of the cast tail.

At the rear end there was a re-style in 1961, a belated nod to the Triumph-led craze for enclosure. There was a new deep rear mudguard, initially fibreglass but by January a steel pressing (much pressed steel was something of an Enfield trademark), which at its front end blended into steel side-section pressings that concealed the top of the suspension units and shrouded the rear sub-frame. A new, plainer seat replaced the previous shapely one, and big chrome lifting handles stuck out of the mudguard on either side. The whole assembly was quickly detachable, but combined with a fuller front mudguard it looked as if the Connie's cowboy nature was being severely diluted. A road test that year described the twin not so much as a roadburner but as "a massive loveable mile-gobbler," which if ridden moderately it truly was. Though strong cross-winds were blamed, top speed was down to 106. There was, however, a belated nod to the Rockers with the fitting of dropped "Ace" handlebars.

The end was in sight for the Connie, however, as Royal Enfield were already working on a radically redesigned and even bigger twin, the 736cc Interceptor. It was principally aimed, like much of the rest of the British industry's output from then on, at the USA, after the bottom had fallen out of the home market from 1960 on. The heart had begun to leak from the old firm too, as Major Smith died in April 1962. For that year, early in the season the swinging-arm bearings changed from bronze to the cheaper Silentbloc. Later, the gearbox mainshaft, the ball-race

and its oil-thrower cap were modified, and the primary chain tensioner, whose mounting bolt could pull out of the alloy of the inner chaincase, was also modified, along with the alternator stator fixings, possibly with those chaincase "big bangs" in mind.

The Constellation's end in 1963 was ignominious for a former streetfighter. As the Interceptor was launched, the Super Meteor was dropped, and the Connie took over its duties as a dray for sidecars, a rapidly diminishing market in the face of cheap small cars. It now featured coil ignition, 7.25:1 compression, power down to 40bhp at 5500 rpm, a single carburettor, lowered gearing, big 3.50 x 19 tyres front and rear, tougher clutch springs, and sidecar gearing and suspension including a sidecar-trail front fork. The final ignominy was the chrome going from the tank along with the polychromatic Burgundy or Peacock Blue finish; now it was cream-painted tank panels and Flame Red for the mudguards and the rest.

A couple of hundred sold before the curtain came down for the Constellation. Like Marlon Brando's character in *On the Waterfront*, it could have been a contender, but the policies and personalities of the well-respected company it had sprung from had made sure that this was not so.

The "Suicide Club" poster boy on his 1958 Constellation WUL 798, which today is on show at the Ace Café.

TECHNICAL SPECIFICATIONS: 1958 ROYAL ENFIELD CONSTELLATION

Capacity	692cc
Bore	70mm
Stroke	90mm
Compression	8.5:1
Power output	51bhp@6250rpm
Electrical system	6 volt
Ignition	Magneto
Generator	Alternator
Wheels and tyres	F: 3.25x19. R: 3.50x19
Brakes	F: dual 6-inch. R: single 7-inch
Weight (dry)	403lbs
Max speed	116mph

CHAPTER 6:
BSA A10
ROCKET GOLD STAR

"I had a 650 Super Rocket – well, it was a '55 Shooting Star frame with a late Rocket engine fitted with the usual mods – Spitfire cam, big valve head and 9.0:1 compression… We had plenty of burn-ups – every run in fact. One I recall was coming back from Norwich on a Sunday afternoon, we were racing a Vauxhall Cresta down the Acle straight and at around the ton, my mate Tony on his Dunstall Dominator started to overtake it. Then I went past both of them, in the gutter on the opposite side of the road…"

Gold Star specialist Phil Pearson

The Rocket Gold Star was arguably the top gun roadster from the giant of Small Heath. The BSA factory in Birmingham East had once built one in four of all the world's motorcycles, with their post-war production peaking in 1948 at 143,000. In 1962 they took what was arguably the best all-round parallel twin, and made it go a little faster and, crucially for the Rocker ethos, look a lot better. This was achieved by visually and mechanically referencing the iconic Gold Star, in a machine that was more tractable than the tough single – and much easier to start. The only pity was that they hadn't done

1963 BSA Rocket Gold Star Clubmans

RGS Clubmans' detailing was superb.

this sooner, and that relatively few would be made.

The production total appears to have been just 1584, and that included 272 export scrambler versions, marketed on the US West Coast as the "650 Gold Star Spitfire Scrambler". The Rocket Gold Star (RGS) came towards the end of the Rocker heyday, commencing in February 1962 and finishing in September 1963, and was produced in tandem with the new unit-construction 650 A65 twin (showing the latter up in the process). It may have been simply a way of using up existing pre-unit and Gold Star parts, and its genesis, as we shall see, undoubtedly was connected with US competition. But in Clubmans trim, with clip-ons, the RRT2 close-ratio gearbox, rear-sets and the "twittering" Gold Star silencer all available as factory extras, and a separate headlamp plus twinned instruments, the A10 RGS was unarguably a Rocker icon. Aesthetics are subjective, but to me this was a beautiful motorcycle.

Its engine was derived from the existing 650 Super Rocket (SR) sports twin, but with higher compression 9.0:1 pistons against the SR's 8.25:1. It claimed an output of 46bhp at 6250 rpm against the Super Rocket's 43bhp, and this was raised to a claimed 50bhp with the Goldie-type silencer fitted. In combination with a dry weight which at 395lbs was nearly 25lbs less than the SR, it is unsurprising to read that one of Duckworth's subjects, Tony Hobbs, who owned an RGS from new, found the BSA "a bit slower pulling away because of the high first gear, but once it got going it could beat most things," including, he said, the Norton 650SS; and it was "easily 10 mph faster" than its A10 Road Rocket (RR) and Super Rocket (SR) predecessors. Road tests saw 105mph with the standard silencer, but Gold Star specialist Eddie Dow, very much part of the RGS story, found that his rider Brian Cox on a Rocket Goldie tuned for production racing

achieved a timed 124mph at MIRA.

Probably more Rockers owned and modified Road Rockets and Super Rockets than they did the RGS, with its limited production run and a 1962/63 base price of £323 8s (with around another £60, five to six weeks' wages then, for all the extras). The Super Rocket was £20 less, and you could get a fully equipped Triumph T120 Bonneville for £309. But the SR came with BSA's second, uninspiring attempt at a headlamp cowling, as found on the cooking A10 Golden Flash, along with the latter's heavy, painted, full-touring mudguards. The cowling, as with Royal Enfield's casquette and Triumph's nacelle, prohibited the fitting of clip-on handlebars.

More than that, BSA in general, including their twins, had a major image problem to contend with. In Banbury where Eddie Dow had his shop there was also a Triumph agency run by Bert Shorey, and Dow's mechanic John Gleed recalled that "A10s got a more mature rider – the kids would go to Bert Shorey's and buy a Bonneville, but the A10 was a nicer bike to ride." It was top of the heap as a sidecar tug, and BSA's Fifties' range – the little Bantam two-stroke which everybody learned on, the pre-unit B31 single, that supremely forgiving-of-neglect ride-to-work bike, the M21 600cc sidevalves which powered the familiar yellow AA outfits – were all worthy, workaday and well-engineered, and all fatally un-sexy.

BORN IN THE USA?

This had its roots historically in 1921 when all six BSA-entered machines retired from the Senior TT with engine trouble, jeopardising the company's decade-long reputation for reliability. Management vowed they would never go racing again. The attitude, and a conservative approach in general, persisted after WW2; development engineer Roland Pike recalled

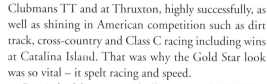

Competition-bred Rocket Goldie looked like a thoroughbred, and was.

RGS could be bend-swung with confidence.

Small Heath's Managing Director James Leek repeating more than once, "Don't let us be pioneers." But contesting trials and scrambles was a different matter, and eventually, as we have seen in Chapter 3, resulted in the glorious all-rounder that was the Gold Star, which then did go (production) racing in the

Clubmans TT and at Thruxton, highly successfully, as well as shining in American competition such as dirt track, cross-country and Class C racing including wins at Catalina Island. That was why the Gold Star look was so vital – it spelt racing and speed.

But it had been special alloy-engined A7 500cc twins (500 because the American sport's governing AMA body dictated that capacity limit for ohv engines, to protect the home-grown Harleys), in light rigid frames, which had taken advantage in 1954 of a brief window of opportunity at the prestigious Daytona Beach races. The window was between the AMA prohibition that year of overhead camshaft engines like the previously winning Norton International, and the full flowering of the powerful Harley-Davidson KR 750 sidevalve vee-twin racers.

The A7 engine had originally been designed by Bert Hopwood in 1950 as a scaled-down version of his A10 650 twin, but until then in competition had suffered from crankshaft breakages. Development had recently cured this, and for 1954 BSA took the first five places at Daytona, although ironically the winner, Bobby Hill, a demon racer of Indian sidevalve twins, had been a late entry who had been found a twin in a Gold Star Clubmans-type swinging-arm frame (twin engines would go into singles' frames, but not vice-

*Feel the noise. 1963
BSA Rocket Gold
Clubmans – top twin?*

versa), rather than one of the works rigid ones (which the AMA had tried to disqualify). Dick Klamforth was second on a works twin, with Gold Stars third, fourth and fifth. As we shall see, the development work done on these engines, and particularly their alloy heads, would feed into the ultimate 650 roadster.

Meanwhile the 650 was already in contention on America's West Coast. The earliest production sporting version of the A10 was Feb 1953's export-only Super Flash. Housed in that year's plunger frame was a 42bhp version of the old engine with the bolted-up gearbox, featuring 8.0:1 compression pistons, larger valves, a sports camshaft, a triplex rather than the regular duplex primary chain, and an Amal TT9 carburettor. The swinging-arm frame and its separate-gearbox motor was waiting in the wings for the twins for 1954; but it is probable that the plunger Super Flash was offered to satisfy US homologation laws, which required a certain number of machines to be produced before they became eligible for American racing classes, something that was wanted immedi-ately. Hap Alzina, the BSA West Coast chief, may have received machines with an even hotter camshaft and higher compression. This 650 was capable of a genuine 110mph, and while I am no enemy of BSA's plunger frame, doing 110 on one would definitely be

Neat factory rear-sets and reversed gear lever for Clubmans RGS.

Footrest folded up to allow use of kickstart.

pushing the outside of the envelope! Less than 700 of the Super Flash appear to have been produced.

Luckily BSA's excellent all-welded swinging-arm frame as introduced on the Gold Star the previous year, was brought in for 1954, and housed the next sports 650, the A10 Road Rocket (RR), although this model would not be available in the UK until June 1956. While not quite as quick as the hairy Super Flash, the redesigned engine, in the swinging-arm frame with its separate gearbox, reverted from a duplex to a single row primary chain, adjusted no longer by a slipper tensioner but by moving the box backwards; under racing stresses, as with the Triumph, it could sometimes slide forward on its mountings. The separate box meant that, as on the Gold Star which had also adopted it, a full range of internal ratios could be offered, including the legendary close-ratio RRT2. Also as on the Goldie, the box could take a reverse camplate to allow for reversing the gear pedal when rear-set footrests were fitted, without altering the familiar (unless you were a Triumph rider) up-for-first shift pattern. The Road Rocket's standard gearing vwas higher than the stock A10's.

The 40bhp Road Rocket featured an alloy cylinder head, with the angle and sweep of both the inlet and exhaust ports differing from the A10's iron head. The valve springs, collars and collets also were different, with the collets retained by a semi-circular groove, and the top collars stronger. Early versions of the head had a bolt-on inlet manifold, with the down-draught angle of the carburettor less than the later version with its one-piece cast-in manifold. The four

The word is "handsome".

A single big Monobloc carb saved a lot of grief balancing twin instruments.

corner studs for the rocker box were longer when fitted to the alloy head, with special sleeve nuts being used at the rear. A TT9 carb was fitted, and compression was again 8.0:1.

Along with the Road Rocket, for 1954 came a 500 sports twin, the new 32bhp alloy-head A7 Shooting Star. This handsome model, finished in polychromatic green, with a dark green frame until 1958, and its 4-gallon chromed tank bearing Gold Star-sized large round badges in black, was well-loved by the discerning. They knew that its top speed in the mid-90s was in practical terms the A10's equal, and revelled in what the late Titch Allen called "its exceptionally flexible and responsive mid-range". But though the Shooting Star's merits were recognized, 500cc was not an attractive prospect for younger

A10RR Road Rocket. Separate headlamp, chromed guards and twinned instruments, but you can see why the sports 650's look needed Gold Star input.

Another piece of Eddie Dow kit in place, "Superleggera" alloy fork yoke meant two-way damping inside, and a fork rebound problem solved.

riders, when they could have a 650.

The A7SS featured an alloy cylinder head, fruit of the Daytona racing development. Unlike Royal Enfield, production BSAs did not experience problems with iron barrel/alloy head sealing. Roland Pike told how, in the run-up to Daytona, a problem with the alloy heads expanding with heat caused stretched or broken cylinder head bolts. In the Development shop they discovered that the bolts' weakest point, and where they broke, was at the root of their last thread into the iron cylinder; by modifying the bolt they eliminated the problem permanently, with the bolts now able to stretch when the head expanded and return to their original length as the head cooled down.

In other areas of the head, while the shrunk-in valve seats on the alloy head proved no problem, the bronze inserts for the spark plugs tended to come out when the plugs were removed. Pike suggested using longer-reach plugs screwing directly into the head, and this worked. Finally, experiments discovered little benefit from the fitting of twin carburettors, except when racing on open pipes. Consequently the shape of the inlet tract was improved, with the port volume found to be critical, until more power was actually derived from a single large carburettor. Which is how production BSA pre-unit twins, including the RGS, would stay until the end, eliminating the chore of carb balancing for owners.

Meanwhile on the West Coast importer Hap Alzina, the man who had faced down the AMA to get the winning A7s entered at Daytona 1954, had a large and continuing input into the sports twin development. He had already organised an attempt at Bonneville on the Class C record for standard

machines, with an unfaired tweaked A7, which took it at 123.49mph; and on the less restrictive Class A record, taken with a stripped A10 running on alcohol with a flying mile of 143.54mph. (In the UK Fred Rist, one of the BSA trio who had won the Maudes Trophy in 1952 on A7 Star Twins, ran a rigid A10 on methanol for sand-racing which was said to be good for 140mph.)

From the mid-Fifties onwards, desert racing, with no 500cc upper limit, boomed out West, leading to the success of Triumph's TR6 650 and machines modified to resemble it. The Cactus Derby, the 500-

You can see why the lads wanted this layout.

Worthy sibling to A10 Rocket Gold Star, 1956 500cc A7 alloy-head Shooting Star.

American-bred A10 Spitfire Scrambler for 1959. It featured standard A10 cycle parts, unlike the '57 Spitfire with Gold Star frame and style.

mile Greenhorn enduro and the 150-mile Big Bear Run all attracted huge fields. Alzina pitched in, and the result for February-September 1957 was the export-only A10 Spitfire Scrambler (SS). The significance of this for our story is that '57's first series of A10 Spitfires have some claim, advanced by the American owner of one, Prof Charles Falco, to be "the first Rocket Gold Star"! This is not so far-fetched, since in essence the SS comprised a Gold Star frame and cycle parts with a tuned Super Rocket engine (once again

Final touch. Eddie Dow "Duetto" twin leading shoe front anchor meant this BSA stopped as well as it went.

the American and other export markets had got the latest sporting twin motor first, with the Super Rocket and its strengthened engine only being released in the UK for 1958).

The 1957 650cc/40 cu in Spitfire Scrambler was a pure off-road blaster, with no lights, speedometer or silencers. Its twin open exhausts were at low level, kicking up a little to terminate towards the bottom of the suspension units. Finished in Nutley Blue, it featured a Gold Star Catalina frame, without frame loops to carry passenger footrests, and complete with the tell-tale kink in the right bottom frame rail to accommodate the singles' oil pump. It carried the Gold Star's chromed mudguards front and rear, its single-sided 8-inch front brake in a half-width hub, and the larger spindle and Goldie fork sliders to take it. Likewise at the rear it featured the Gold Star "crinkle-hub" QD rear wheel and rod-operated 7-inch brake which the Gold Star swinging-arm with its smaller pivot bolt permitted. The brake pedal pivoted from a boss bolted through the left-hand frame tube.

In the engine, Hap Alzina, as well as specifying 9.0:1 or higher compression pistons, had evidently experimented to find the best mix for the job. Roland Pike rated Alzina's engineering ability highly, judging that the East Coast importer, expatriate Alf Childs, was "a great promoter...but...he did not understand motorcycles as well as Hap Alzina," who Pike said provided much additional support for the factory's design and technical departments wherever he could. A late March 1957 West Coast Press release stated: "Original projection on the Spitfire Scrambler was that a special scrambles camshaft would be most applicable for the basic purpose of the machine. However, careful dynamometer and road testing disclosed extraordinarily satisfactory performance with the full-race camshaft and hence this fitment has been adopted as a standard component" – that was Part No. 67-357, known thereafter as the Spitfire cam.

The Spitfire's gearbox for '57 only was the SCT2, SC denoting scrambles, and the T2 signifying, as it did with the RRT2, the double use of Torrington needle roller bearings. These internals would be dropped for the following year due to the fact that, while ideal for tarmac racing, they proved less suitable for dirt and desert. Alzina had also introduced the stronger W and S valve springs with special keepers and collets, already proved on the Gold Star, as an option for the big BSA twins. They were one of 31 items, including the camshaft and alloy cylinder head, not listed in the stock parts catalogue but itemised in a separate early 1958 bulletin. Aftermarket twin-carb conversions were also available. Despatched from

Small Heath as the "A10 Rocket Scrambler", some 350 1957 Spitfire Scramblers were built, with unique frame number prefixes of CA7A. The relatively low numbers probably reflect the fact that, as with the Triumph TR6, many desert racers preferred to buy secondhand machines and modify them themselves.

After 1957 the connection with the Rocket Gold Star weakens, as the "second series" A10 scramblers running from January 1958 to July 1959 used standard A10 frames, forks, brakes, etc – even fitting the centre stand! Gearboxes became SCT, finish was Flamboyant Red, and the twinned exhaust pipes were carried high, on the left side. The frame was claimed to be "lightweight", but one specialist scoffed that all they did to lighten it was cut off one of the lugs for the toolbox, using the other as a mounting for the exhaust system. Nevertheless the Spitfire scramblers were competitive, with one winning the East Coast scrambles championship for 1960.

The reason for the reversion to the stock A10 cycle parts may perhaps be found in Pike's remark about export bikes: "On the factory floor [they were] not appreciated. Anything special was a nuisance, it was

an uphill job" to get it made. Edward Turner was now in overall charge, and his wish to promote Triumph's TR6 may also have been a factor. After some 390 had been built, there was a third series, from September 1959 to September 1962, finished in Nutley Blue again until the 1962 model year; they were similar, and numbered around 622. After that they became the genuine scrambler versions of the Rocket Gold Star, which we'll look at later.

1962 Rocket Gold Star with BSA handlebars, chromed headlamp "ears", plus 8-inch single leading shoe front brake.

Rocket in the rain.
1962 model on test.

BSA
650 SUPER ROCKET

TWIN CYLINDER MODEL A10 SR

"When you hear that big engine humming under you you just want to yell "Hallelujah!" It's more than a thrill, it's a wonderful experience."

£303
including £50. 10s.
purchase tax

At the summit of the Andes 14,000 ft. above sea level between Chile and Argentina.

Its improved alloy cylinder head with high compression pistons and sports camshaft put the "Super Rocket" in the world-beater class. With a specially tuned, bench-tested engine, this 650 cc machine is built for safety and speed.

Engine. 646 cc (70 × 84 mm.) O.H.V. Pressure oil feed to rocker mechanism; high performance camshaft; aluminium alloy cylinder head with pistons giving compression ratio of 8¼ to 1; crankshaft drive-side supported by roller bearing, timing side by lead-bronze bush; crankshaft of immense strength, light alloy connecting rods with micro-babbitt big-end liners; single camshaft, with drive gear to magneto; dry sump lubrication with double-gear type oil pump; oil tank 5½ pints; twin absorption silencers.

Carburettor. Amal Monobloc type of large bore; large capacity air cleaner extra; twist grip throttle; air slide operated by lever on offside under dual seat.

Transmission. B.S.A. 4-speed gearbox with positive stop foot control; gear ratios 4.55–6.0–7.4–13.1, optional internal gear ratios available; multi-plate fabric clutch with cable adjustment on handlebar; primary chain ⅜ × .305" with double-cam cush drive on engine shaft; primary chain oil-bath inspection cap for rapid clutch spring adjustment; rear chain ⅝ × ⅜" with a guard over the top run.

Ignition and Lighting. Lucas magneto with manually controlled advance and retard mechanism; separate chain driven 6-volt C.V.C. dynamo; headlamp with pre-focus light unit and pilot light; illuminated speedometer and electric horn; stop and tail lamp incorporating rear reflector; 13 amp. hr. battery.

Fuel Capacity. 4 gallons.

Tyres. Dunlop 3.25—19 ribbed front, and 3.50—19 Universal rear.

Brakes. Full width hubs with high-grade cast-iron drums; straight spokes; brakes 8" diameter front and 7" diameter rear with floating shoes; finger adjustment to both brakes, front on handlebar.

Suspension. B.S.A. hydraulically damped telescopic front forks; hydraulically damped swinging-arm rear suspension, adjustable for weight in three positions. Alternative strengths of suspension springs available.

Frame. Duplex tubular cradle with provision for sidecar attachments; easy-action roll-on central stand; front stand; key operated steering head lock; quickly detachable rear wheel; new dome section mudguards without front stay. B.S.A. dual seat, with pillion footrests.

Finish. Royal red or Princess grey. Frame black; brake cover plates polished; chromium-plated petrol tank; chromium wheel rims and front hub cover plate; polished primary chaincase, gearbox and timing covers; bright parts chromium-plated. Alternative colour, black. Attractive plastic tank badges.

General Dimensions. Wheelbase 56"; ground clearance 6"; overall length 85"; dry weight 413 lb.

Extra Fittings. (Prices include P.T.) Legshields £4. 14s. 10d.; Safety bars £6. 5s. 9d.; Handrail £2. 1s. 2d.; Prop stand £1. 6s. 3d.; Rear chaincase giving total enclosure £3. 9s. 11d.; Carrier, to special order; Air cleaner £1. 5s. 10d.; Rev. counter £8. 1s. 6d.; Chromium-plated mudguards £4. 15s. 2d.

Siamesed exhaust pipes, as illustrated, supplied only to order.

1963 A10 Super Rocket, alloy-headed mechanical basis of the faster, more charismatic Rocket Goldie.

BORN IN BANBURY?

Meanwhile in 1958 for the UK, the A10 had undergone really significant changes which would make it, in Super Rocket form, fit to power the Rocket Goldie.

Originally, for 1950, Bert Hopwood had thoroughly redesigned an existing A7 500 twin into a 650, which was then also reduced to a new 500. With engine cooling and mechanical quietness much in mind, he created what Pike called "a good rugged engine." It featured a single rear-mounted chain-driven camshaft, and pushrods in cast-in tubes angled forwards; a rare A10/A7 irritation was that there was no easy way to refit them, even using the special pushrod fitting plate or "comb," which held the pushrods in the correct position while the one-piece rocker box was lowered into place. The one-piece forged crankshaft, with its flywheel threaded on and then bolted to the centre web, ran on a roller drive side main bearing, and for rigidity, a long plain timing side bearing, with its journal induction-hardened, ground and polished. This plain bush, which also fed

oil to the big ends, would cause trouble for the A10's unit successor, the A65; but A10 owner, journalist and VMCC founder the late Titch Allen wrote that "no A7 or A10 I have ever known has ever called for a replacement of the [roller] main ball race, [and] given clean oil, the [timing side plain bush] had from new a very long life." Regular oil changes every 1000 to 1500 miles were a must, though.

The crankshaft carried alloy con rods with long-wearing renewable big end shells, steel-backed and of lead-bronze with indium flash diffused into their surfaces, in contrast to Triumph's plain white metal bearing. The BSA twin always used the same gear-driven oil pump, even for racing, with no troubles. Putting the engine breather on the end of the camshaft ensured that it was properly timed, and BSA pre-unit twins were less prone to oil leaks than some others. Parallel twin vibration was inevitably present, but throughout the rev range, not in particular periods. Capable of six-figure mileages without a major rebuild, these engines had a justified reputation for durability – as long as they were not over-revved, i.e. not beyond an absolute maximum of 6000rpm. This was more than adequate for fast road work, and the sports 500 crankshaft had been strengthened effectively for 1954. But in the heat of American competition rev limits were not always adhered to, with occasional crank breakages still resulting, especially for the 650 with its longer stroke.

So for 1958, with UK Production racing also on the rise, the A10 engine was revised for yet greater strength so that it could be safely tuned for higher outputs. A new one-piece forged crankshaft of EN16B steel emerged from the BSA forges. Its load capacity was increased, with the big end bearing shell made more substantial. The new crankshaft now had its flywheel located in a circular central boss by means of three radial set-screws, rather than bolted on laterally as before. The crank throw was hollow and contained an improved sludge trap, positioned end-wise and prevented from rotating by an extension of one of the flywheel set-screws.

Eddie Dow's mechanic John Gleed considered that "on the road at the time, the BSA twins' 1958-on crankshaft was indestructible." The engine's breather-valve was also improved. Finally, the cylinder base flange, as an external identifier, was made half an inch thicker. These "thick flange" motors, with DA10 engine prefixes (CA10R for the Super Rocket until 1960), were the basis of the BSA 650's final burst of glory. They could be revved safely to 6500-6700rpm.

There was little further development. For 1960 the carburettor size increased, with the A10 going from the 1¹⁄₁₆-inch Amal 376 Monobloc to the export Super

Rocket's 1⅛-inch 389, and the home Super Rocket to a 1½₂-inch 389, which Eddie Dow considered ideal. At the same time, the inlet tract and inlet valve size were increased to suit.

Down in Banbury were Taylor-Dow, the successful Gold Star specialists run by Capt Eddie Dow, winner of the 1955 500 Senior Clubmans TT. John Gleed characterised Dow as "a thinker," who was beginning to realise that "we'd sell a lot more [Gold Stars] if they weren't relatively difficult to start. So he began thinking," especially as they were already selling A10s and Super Rockets.

The latter were crying out for a more sporting appearance, as well as better brakes. The 1958 revisions had seen a couple of unwelcome Triumph-originated changes, with the A10's previous "frog-eye" headlamp cover, and the Road Rocket's separate headlamp, which had permitted twinned instruments, both being replaced by a tidier but not very attractive or accessible cowling. And the twins' brakes, Super Rocket included, had changed from the nice-looking Ariel-type all-alloy full-width hub 7-inch items front and rear, to Triumph-style full-width ones with heavier cast-iron hubs, which Titch Allen called "something like a cast-iron saucepan", and which, despite an increased size at the front to 8 inches, featured a distinct fall-off in performance from the Ariel's, which set up correctly had worked well. The new 7-inch rear drum, also cast-iron, was still cable-operated, and replaced the previous excellent QD hub. (The one welcome input from Triumph would come for 1960, when a BSA weak spot, the slip-prone 6-spring clutch, was replaced by a design with 4 springs like Triumph's, though it still ran wet, against Triumph's dry one.) The Super Rocket was also lumbered with the A10's heavy, fully valanced mudguards. The time was ripe for a change.

Some customers thought so too. On 12 October 1959 Mr D. Mathew, a merchant seaman living at Lime Tree Park, Coventry, ordered a Taylor-Dow Gold Star "with a twin engine". This has been heralded as the birth of the Rocket Goldie, which has been credited as Dow's brainchild. But firstly, as we have seen, the US competition scene had bred something very similar two years previously; and the factory itself was well aware of the possibilities, having already prepared a bike for ex-Triumph works rider Eric Chilton to contest the 1958 ISDT, putting a Road Rocket engine into a Gold Star frame for him. And secondly, as Gleed confirmed to me, "ours were Super Rockets with Goldie bits stuck on."

Eddie Dow has detailed for *Classic Bike* what he did to Mr Matthews' engine (W and S valve springs, 10:1 compression pistons, an RRT2 close-ratio

gearbox) and cycle parts – Goldie spec. fork bottoms (the only element that differed from the standard forks) to allow a 190mm front brake, Gold Star chromed sports mudguards, clip-ons and separate headlamp, tank, seat and "everything else" including a Gold Star swinging-arm plus rear brake and wheel. But John Gleed disputes the latter – "I and another John did the work, so I probably remember it better than Eddie. We never did the Goldie swinging-arm, and I believe we even used the Super Rocket's valanced rear mudguard, but chromed.

"We did no more than 20 conversions from 1960 to '61, and they were all based around brand new Super Rockets. That way we could then sell the discarded bits like the headlamp cowling as new spares, to help keep the costs down, as there wasn't the money about that there is today. So the clue to one of our conversions is that being new bikes, they all had local registrations, with either UW or BW as the last two of their registration letters. Not all of them had all the changes – one might have just clip-ons with the

Rocket Gold Star for 1963, its second and final year. 190mm front brake was standard for '63.

headlamp brackets and separate shell, another, just the fork bottoms and front brake.

"The only conversion we would do on bikes that weren't new was the rear-set footrests, which I did personally. Someone at Dow's knew Al Cave" (the legendary BSA Works Manager), "and Al robbed some Clubmans Gold Star right-side fittings off the line for us! But on the left side of the twin's frame there was a sidecar lug where the rear-set mounting had to go. So I went to the local agricultural engineers and found some large steel washers with a ⅜th-inch hole. I filed a hexagon in one, brazed it over the outside of the sidecar lug, and with a similar one on the inside and an aluminium spacer in the hole, we could fit rear-sets, with the standard rear brake pedal shortened to suit, as on the Clubman Goldie."

Dow the thinker had a purpose in fulfilling this demand and in making the factory aware of the hybrid's potential. As primarily a Gold Star specialist, he was naturally anxious to extend the sports singles' production life for as long as possible. He compiled a list of thirty-odd necessary existing items and took it to Small Heath late in 1959, to emphasise how easily a sports twin could be crafted from what they were already making. But he also suggested that, with relatively minor changes, a frame could be produced which would take both the pre-unit singles, Goldie included, and the twins; with the rationalization hopefully prolonging the life of the Gold Star. However, "at the time," Dow recalled, "BSA were six months behind with deliveries of bikes to the States, and at a sales meeting the idea was dismissed."

Subsequently BSA 1) lost Dow's list, and 2) missed the boat. Dow said of the company mentality, "Here was the obvious choice to make a component that would have a dual purpose, but BSA had their own style of doing things. It was a bit like a computer… because the Rocket Gold Star was a 650, it had to have a 3.50 x 19-inch front wheel, not a 3.00 x 19 (like the Gold Star), etc." So what finally emerged was a special, one-off frame. The factory had phoned Dow two years later to ask if he had kept a copy of the list (he hadn't), and in the meantime 1959's UK sales boom had collapsed. So it is almost certain that, as with the Gold Star, it was American demand which triggered this late pre-unit's creation. After that, as John Gleed said, "We did [no conversions] in 1962, because we'd got the proper thing."

THE REAL DEAL

The A10 Rocket Gold Star was announced for February 1962, with the West Coast off-road version catalogued as the "650 Gold Star Spitfire Scrambler"; in the East they were just the Spitfire Scrambler. All versions were distinguished with a unique frame number, which for the first time ever included the "A10", rather than the usual "A7", in the frame prefix. For 1962 frames commenced at GA10-101, then for 1963 at GA10-390. A few of the scramblers were prefixed GA10A. Rocket Gold Star engines would normally also have "HHC" stamped beneath the engine number to denote their High Compression – 9.0:1 was standard, against the Super Rocket's 8.25:1; although the RGS could also be ordered in Touring trim with the SR pistons, and one was tested by *Motor Cycling* pulling a sidecar!

The special frame prefix was appropriate, since the frame itself was unique. How much attention Rockers at the time paid to this, rather than the Gold Star trappings, is not recorded, but subsequently, as genuine Rocket Goldies have become Holy Grails for BSA fans and collectors, worth at least double the price of even neatly done replicas, the details have become disproportionately significant.

How to tell a genuine RGS frame? It lacked the "kink" in the rails for the single's oil pump. At the front, on the twin downtubes, there were four, instead of the stock two, engine mounting lugs; the extra pair could be welded on an A10 frame later, but the genuine lugs were forged, which close inspection will reveal. As on the Goldie, there was no provision for a steering lock on the top fork yoke and no lug for it to engage with (although very late Super Rockets also lacked this). More importantly, the frame is reinforced at the head tube joint by an extra gusset wrapped right around the front of the steering head. The RGS arrangement appeared to differ from the Gold Star's, which was less substantial and didn't go all the way round. This RGS feature was also apparently shared by the late Super Rockets.

The front fork featured Gold Star-type bottom halves, with sliders which accepted a thread-in spindle, as opposed to the Super Rocket's clamping arrangement. This permitted the fitting of the under-rated standard 8-inch single-sided front brake (later substitutes off an A65 can be detected by their slightly wider linings at 1.62 inches as against the

*BSA Rocket Gold Star
Clubmans, the ultimate A10.*

genuine 1.5 inches). Or as an option there was the famous 190mm full-width hub brake, which Eddie Dow's "Duetto" twin leading shoe conversion could transform from somewhat disappointing to fiercely effective. The fork shrouds were chromed, and beneath them gaiters were fitted.

At the fork top there were two headlamp-mounting styles on offer: with the black lamp carried on chromed pressings from the chromed shrouds; or when the optional clip-ons were fitted, the more sporting Clubman Goldie type with the plug-in QD light carried high and proud on tubular black enamelled stays. The rev counter, driven from the necessarily adapted inner timing case, was at a 3:1 ratio only found on the Super Rocket and RGS; it was an optional extra which most went for. The twinned instruments were rubber-mounted on separate brackets, tilted further back than on the Goldie. The standard handlebars for the UK were a fairly wide, now rare, touring type, but turned down at the ends; for US export, a higher Western bar was fitted.

At the other end of the frame, there were small-diameter drillings in the swinging-arm gusset to accept the smaller Gold Star rear fork, with its

smaller pivot bolt and spindle, which as noted permitted the use of the excellent single-sided "crinkle-hub" QD rear wheel with its rod-operated 7-inch back brake. The Rocket Goldie's brake pedal pivoted from a boss bolted through a small bushed hole in the left side lower frame tube, another RGS frame distinguishing feature. The chrome rear chainguard was as on the Goldie.

Final frame details centred on the footrest arrangements. The rear-set footrests, which folded up so that the kickstart could be used, became standard for '63 when most of the bikes were produced. The mounting lugs for these rear-sets were, uniquely, welded in the loops of tube which braced the rear sub-frame and also took the pillion footrests. They can be added later by fakers, but the lower frame loops, where A10 footrests were normally mounted, were never fitted on the RGS frame, so the tubing should be virgin at that point. However as mentioned, not quite all Rocket Goldies had rear-sets; *Motor Cycling* tested two in 1963, both with A10 footrests, one solo and one pulling a sidecar, which was a bit like putting Shergar between the shafts of a hay wagon. Still, Chris

Canted tank lining and jutting headlamp on tubular mounts gave Clubmans RGS an eager air.

Vincent had just won the 1962 sidecar TT on an A7-powered kneeler outfit…

The model's other distinguishing features are Gold Star accessories, sometimes optional, always handsome. The options included Dunlop alloy rims for the wheels, and an 18-inch rear wheel against the stock 19-inch one; and for the siamesed exhaust system with its hard-to-copy S-shaped link pipe, a "track" Goldie-type silencer in place of the standard BSA sausage-shaped one with a normal tail-pipe. The Goldie type "twittered" on the over-run like the singles', and helped boost output from the standard 46bhp at 6250rpm to 50bhp. The RGS version of this silencer had to mate with the twin's smaller 1½-inch bore exhaust, and featured a separate fixing clamp rather than the Goldie's pinch bolt. Twin exhausts could be specified, but not if rear-sets were to be fitted.

The Rocket Gold Star's crowning glory was its 4-gallon Gold Star petrol tank, complete with butterfly filler cap with a breather pipe curled around it. This magnificent chromed tank was painted matt silver with the panels lined in maroon, and featured the large-diameter round red plastic badges otherwise found only on the Goldie, or in black on the A7SS. There were also optional 5-gallon Lyta alloy tanks for complete Club (or café) racers, but the 4-gallon was the real eye-candy. The RGS's dualseat was as the Super Rocket's, but with altered mountings underneath.

A further option, standard for export, was a 2.5 Imp. gallon chromed tank, also carrying the big badge and finished in handsome metallic red. Americans took to the hot Goldie twin – there was even a Revell plastic model kit of it. Unfortunately the Scramblers, 272 of which were produced, changed to the ASCT gearbox (AS is thought to stand for American Scrambles), which featured an ultra-low trials-type first gear and then a huge jump to the remaining, scrambles gears. One tempting American aftermarket option was a twin-carb conversion. The kit that I saw was smart, with a chromed inlet manifold, polished short bell-mouths, and a Webco remote float chamber extended to the left, its end cover decorated with concentric rings. The carburettors themselves were 376 Monoblocs, quite small at 1¹⁄₁₆-inch – which John Gleed, who had rebuilt that particular engine, approved of, reckoning that the earlier Road Rocket with its smaller

carb had gone better than the subsequent Super Rocket. The kit did not seem to make an appreciable difference to performance, but the bike was still running in so we got nowhere near the upper limits where it might have.

The US connection explains why the RGS's front mudguard sometimes showed a good gap above the tyre, to allow for the fitting of a bigger scrambles 21-inch front wheel, which some favoured.   The mudguards were unique again, with a beaded flare on the forward end of the front one, and on the bottom end of the rear, but no bead along the lower back edge of the front. The back guard mounted a light, open-sided rear light/number plate carrier off a mid-Fifties Bantam. The guards were of chromed steel, and the front one was fixed with a six-bracket arrangement again unique to the model. Both this and the use of steel, where the Goldie's alloy guards would have been lighter, had a practical as well as an aesthetic function.

The strong guards and stays helped counter one of the bike's Achilles' heels. The stock BSA front fork was strong, and more than adequate for normal use on or off-road. But without the rudimentary brace which the guards represented, it could get out of shape at high speed; even then, the stays were prone to fracture. The Beeza fork also featured rebound-only damping, causing the infamous clang on full extension. The classic solution was a Taylor-Dow "Superleggera" conversion, featuring a ball bearing in an aluminium cage with drillings to allow oil to pass through at a controlled rate. The penalty was that, since the conversion restricted the fork's short (3½-

inch) slider movement by another inch, it made for a harsh ride on anything but the smoothest surfaces.

Finally the Rocket Gold Star's engine, aside from the 9.0:1 compression and an optional larger inlet valve for its alloy head, was remarkably standard A10. True, the camshaft, as on the later Super Rockets, was the Spitfire (67-357) profile. And it was said at the time that the best of the bench-tested Super Rocket engines were set aside as Rocket Goldies. But the motor's single Monobloc 389 carburettor, at 1$\frac{5}{32}$-inch, was not much bigger than the Flash's 1$\frac{1}{8}$-inch instrument, and this was probably a major contributor to the engine's excellently unfussy and torquey nature. This stood in contrast to the Clubmans Gold Star, whose lack of low-down urge due to its massive 1½-inch GP carb, as well as starting difficulties, had been prime reasons for creating the more useable hybrid twin in the first place.

And the twin was a direct contrast with the single, for what many Rocket Gold Stars did fit was the Goldie's close-ratio RRT2 gearbox, which on the single had meant clutch-slipping to at least 30mph. The Rocket Goldie's torquier nature reduced – though did not eliminate – the need to slip the clutch on a 650 which, like the Goldie, could see over 60mph in first! Standard overall gearing for the RGS was helped by a 46-tooth rear wheel sprocket which kept lovely fat power where it was needed for the road, between 50 and 90mph. In 1962 the RRT2's close ratios (at 7.92:1 first, 5.96, 4.96 and 4.52) were found to be a bit too close for the twin, and were spaced out a little for 1963 (at 8.39:1 first, 6.34,

5.25, and 4.78). For road use, Eddie Dow recommended changing the engine sprocket from the RGS's standard 23-tooth item (the SR's was 21-tooth) to a 20-tooth one, as the engine tended to be overgeared. A late '62 road test saw "only" 105mph from an RGS in very poor weather, but since Super Rockets had been clocked at 108mph, that is accepted as a realistic top end for the model. As mentioned, Dow's rider Bruce Cox put an RGS through the timing lights at MIRA at 124mph, but almost certainly this involved at least taller gearing.

At the end of the day, what was the Clubman's RGS like? "I thought it was a fantastic machine," Eddie Dow recalled. "I remember we supplied three London boys, café racer types, and they used to come here on Saturday mornings and claim that, riding three abreast, they could hold 120mph up the M1. And I dare say they were right – the Rocket Gold Star had very high gearing…" That did not sit so well with all Rockers. One who had traded in his A7SS for an RGS back in the day ended up regretting it, as he found that while the 650 was great on long runs out of town, the 500 had been more suitable for the kind of round-town burn-ups they mostly did.

For many, though, the squirty yet solid nature of the engine, the fine acceleration, the wonderfully rorty exhaust note from the single silencer with its unmistakable "twitter" on the over-run, the better brakes, the excellent steering and the handling tautening as speeds rose, and the way the Rocket Goldie would effortlessly do everything in third (including 100mph) that an A10 did in top, all produced a peak experience, over-riding the fiddliness of any clutch slipping with the RRT2 and the discomfort, except at speed, of the clip-on/rear-set riding position.

Though as Mike Clay confirmed, BSA sports 650s gained a reputation for ruggedness and longevity, it should not be forgotten that if ridden as intended i.e. hard, like all their contemporaries they were high maintenance machines. Journalist Dave Minton ran a 1961 Super Rocket with 9000 miles on it when he got it, and reckoned that for him and his like-minded friends taking high-speed weekend runs, the BSA required the equivalent of a day's spannering for every day of fast riding, in addition to regular chores like the vital oil changes.

In 40,000 miles the 650, its engine tuned to RGS spec., never seriously let him down, and that included a final stint pulling a sidecar. But oil tank seams split, head-steadies cracked, the points in the magneto as well as the slip ring, brushes, etc, required regular attention and renewal, and the valve springs, which would be ruined if you dropped down a gear at high revs, needed replacing several times. Rear chains,

however, lasted tens of thousands of miles thanks to BSA'a superbly progressive transmission shock absorber; and overall, though the constant fettling became irritating, the A10 SR was "wholly reliable" where it counted.

In production racing the Rocket Gold Star did not excel. At Thruxton in 1962, one entered by Syd Lawton failed to thrive, and the entry John Gleed was spannering for was doing well until the long bolt and stud that held the magneto on came out, though luckily it dropped on top of the gearbox – "I think it was the vibration at high revs made it shake like a tuning fork," said John. The delay relegated them to fourth in class. In 1963 Dave Williams and top rider Ron Langston, on one of the three RGS entries, set a lap record, wearing away the frame rail underneath the gearbox with hard cornering, and were lying third when they were sidelined with a split oil union, and had to settle for sixth in class.

Gleed recounted how, with the 1962 entry in the pits, "The bike was so hot that it was a while before we could work on it, we had to throw buckets of water over it. Thruxton in summer used to get so hot, all the oil in a Goldie's primary chaincase would dry out and you could end up with no teeth on the sprocket. Thruxton really sorted the men from the boys. Sorted the machines, too." With the A65 in production and the RGS on a limited, finite run, it was unlikely that discreet factory support, as previously provided for the Gold Stars, would have been forthcoming.

The Rocket Goldie bowed out in Sept 1963, though a few more oddball machines would be built using leftover RGS parts, with some rumoured to feature regular A7 frames. Sadly the A65, though a sturdy touring engine, was to be beset by well-documented troubles (timing side main bearing failures, "rogue" spark, etc), as well as an uncharismatic appearance. So the Rocket Gold Star really was the handsome high point in terms of the parallel twins from Small Heath.

TECHNICAL SPECIFICATIONS: 1962 BSA A10 ROCKET GOLDSTAR

Capacity	646cc
Bore	70mm
Stroke	84mm
Compression	9.0:1
Power output	46bhp@6250rpm
Electrical system	6 volt
Ignition	Magneto
Generator	Dynamo
Wheels and tyres	F: 3.25x19. R: 3.50x19
Brakes	F: 8-inch. R: 7-inch
Weight (dry)	395lbs
Max speed	108mph

CHAPTER 7:
NORTON DOMINATOR 650SS

"I tuned the bike (a 1956 Dominator 99) with go-faster bits from the 650SS, all lightened, polished and balanced, and very carefully put together. At first I was disappointed that after all that work, it would still only do 85, flat out, chin on the tank. Then I fitted a rev counter, and realised that when it was flat out it was only doing 4,000 rpm. So I took another fistful of throttle. The bike took off like a rocket, right up to and past 100, and I damn near fell off it. So I fitted a quick-action throttle and rode on the rev counter instead of the noise and vibrations…From my home in Bristol to my digs in Oxford became one long racetrack"

Mike Sewell

1962 650SS. Hunky!

I t was a strange thing. Norton had followed the Triumph-inspired craze for rear enclosure panels and two-tone colour schemes, first on their "Light" Jubilee/Navigator unit twins, and then from 1960 on the bigger pre-unit 500 and 600 Dominators. This often involved lower halves (frame and stands included) in impractical Dove Grey, or in the primary colour, which could be red, or blue. It was understandable – the company had been surprised how quickly 1959 twins finished optionally all in red or in metallescent blue had sold. This new garishness seemed to be what people wanted. Yet…

Then for 1962 in the UK came Norton's first 650 twins, the range leading with the twin carb 650SS, and the madness stopped there, stopped dead. The 650SS petrol tank was in the silver habitually associated with Norton, the full mudguards chrome, at first as an option but standard the following year, and the rest black. In the Norton tradition, this was unpretentious, purposeful-looking, and with an unmistakably masculine aura compared with Triumph's almost delicate lightness.

The tubes of its Featherbed frame were sturdy, and the Norton's horizontal lines were arrow-straight – the tank bottom, running into the seat base, the horizontal grab handles, the base-line of the exhaust and silencer, the three horizontal ribs on the oil tank, and the base of the long, spiked, tapering chrome tank badges. Combined with the aggressively steep angle of the Roadholder front forks and their wide-set, substantial stanchions and alloy sliders, this was a bike which if you looked at it properly was as taut as an archer's shaft awaiting release. Riders recognized this immediately: the 650SS was voted Machine of the Year by *Motorcycle News* readers that year, and the next.

Vic Willoughby putting 1962 650SS through its paces.

1962 Norton

The World's Best Road Holder

1962 650SS, with determined rider and optional siamesed exhaust.

power and top speed. The only reason to build a Triton now, apart from the fun of it, was because not enough of the 650SS were made, and they cost 10% more than the Triumph. Mick Gower, a 650 Triton rider from the enthusiasts' Salt Box café by Biggin Hill, told Duckworth that he could never pass his hard-riding mate's 650SS.

Norton's superiority in the handling department was already well known. Now its overall supremacy was hammered home with three years' successive wins at Thruxton by "the Lawton Norton," as famous in its day as the Trident proddie racer Slippery Sam would become ten years later.

DOMINATION DEVELOPED

Behind every great bike there's a great designer, and in this case there were two – or to be fair, three. The original Norton twin engine had been laid out, starting in 1947, by the great Bert Hopwood. The engine in 1952 was then put in roadsters with the state-of-the-art Featherbed frame, fruit of the inventive genius of Ulsterman Rex McCandless, who with his brother Cromie had developed his ideas from swinging-arm conversions to a complete all-welded chassis which they sold to Norton. Then at the end of the Fifties the engine was transformed into a true sportster by Hopwood's colleague and collaborator, development engineer Doug Hele.

The first 497cc Dominator motor had been conceived very much with a view to avoiding perceived weaknesses in the great original, Triumph's Speed Twin. Hopwood had worked with Edward Turner at Ariel and Triumph, and was well aware of the Triumph 500's proneness to overheating, particularly at the cylinder head; its tendency to leak oil; and the way its gear-driven twin camshafts condemned it, in Hopwood's view, to be "fundamentally a rattler".

Hopwood's own ideal had to be trimmed to Norton's limited facilities. The name might still be famous for racing success, but the Bracebridge Street, Birmingham factory was small, and its machinery, bar that used exclusively for the works racers, was antiquated. Hopwood had wanted a one-piece crankshaft, not the production three-piece type; a die-cast not a sand-cast engine; and an alloy not an iron head. In addition the design had to fit in the existing plunger-framed cycle parts of the ES2 single.

Hopwood opted for a single chain-driven camshaft located at the front of the engine. The pushrod

Appearances were not deceptive, either. *Motor Cycling* journalist Bruce Main-Smith tested the new machine very hard and thoroughly, with wet weather ton-plus laps of MIRA, one-way runs of 119.5mph, and road trips from one end of the M1 to the other (the motorway terminated in the Midlands then) at a steady 90mph. Offering 49bhp at 6800rpm, the new kid on the block aced the 46bhp Bonnie on both

The Bert Hopwood-designed Norton 500 twin, here for 1954 in Model 7 form, with less expensive single downtube swinging-arm frame, which from 1953 was produced alongside the Featherbed.

Tops for handling already, 1962 650SS gave Norton the speed to truly dominate.

tunnels were cast-in at the front of the cylinder block, avoiding Triumph's separate exterior pushrod tunnel there, which obscured air-flow back over the engine as well as famously leaking oil. There were air-spaces between the Norton barrels, as well as transversely between the bores and the tunnels. The iron cylinder head continued the good cooling theme via excellent air-flow over the splayed exhaust valves and wide-set exhaust ports. Vertical finning around them encouraged cooling air to pass between the ports. The inlet ports were closer together, but slightly offset to promote induction swirl.

Magneto ignition, and pressed steel primary chaincase which sealed better than most.

Inside the head, steeply angled valves meant a notably shallow combustion chamber and avoided the limitation of the Triumph twins' deep chambers and wide valve angles; the importance of this in terms of tuning potential would emerge later. The head featured integral rocker boxes, with the rockers accessed by a rectangular cover at the rear. This eliminated another Triumph oil leak hot spot, the rocker box joints, but would contribute to a downside of the Norton twin, the relative difficulty of working on it. The alloy con rods featured separate steel-backed shell big end bearings, which Triumph with their white metal bearings would only adopt in 1956.

Two further fundamentals distinguished the Norton engine from the Triumph. First, Hopwood designed in a strong bottom end, with the crank running on large timing side ball journal and drive side roller main bearings. The dimensions of these would stay the same with no major problems until the 1972 Norton Commando, although the timing side would prove the weaker on tuned, larger engines ridden hard; and Norton racer and special builder Paul Dunstall felt that the Dominator was handicapped in race terms by what he considered small

main bearings. But for road use they performed very well, particularly compared to pre-1954 Triumphs, on which as Titch Allen wrote, "10,000 miles was considered good in the early Fifties" for the life of a 650 Triumph's drive side ball race main before it needed replacing. Secondly, the Norton's 66 x 72.6 dimensions, while not over-square, were shorter-stroked than the Triumph and BSA competition, which made for good power, rigidity and consequent oil-tightness.

Existing Norton components included the excellent double gear oil pump in the timing chest, driven via a pinion from the crankshaft. The Norton gearbox was also one of the best in the business. The pressed steel primary chaincase, like all of them, could leak if abused, but was better than most. Released as the Model 7 for 1949 (by which time Hopwood had left the company), but soon known as the Dominator, the 29bhp single-carb 500 twin was a success for the company, becoming known as reliable and tractable. It was relatively heavy at 413lbs against the 5T with Spring Wheel at around 400lbs, and it was pricier; a 1950 Model 7 cost £221 compared with a 5T at £185. That price difference would remain.

The Norton was, as mentioned, difficult to work

on, compared to Triumph where the valves could be adjusted without removing the tank; because of the integral rocker boxes, the Norton's cylinder head had to come off to work on the valves, and there were some inaccessible nuts and bolts recessed into holes cut into the fins of the block. Adjusting the cam chain was also difficult, as an apparently perfectly tensioned chain would then go humming taut when the timing case cover was replaced. Correct alignment of all four pushrods was tricky, and a de-coke could be an all-day job. The rear chain was on the puny side at ⅝ x ¼ inch, and this would not be remedied until 1965! If the engine itself had a weakness, it was a potential for the spigot in the head-to-barrel joint to break up – though in the experience of journalist Bruce Main-Smith, this did not seem to matter!

1952 brought the Featherbed frame for the 500 twin. Versions so equipped were known as the Dominator 88 De-Luxe, not to be confused with the later, rear-panelled models. The frame had already given Norton's ohc racers a new lease of life. Racing frames were in superior Reynolds 531 tubing, while the roadster twins were in 14-gauge "B" tubing. They were sif-bronze welded, a method which allowed welds to be precisely built up in fillets, and since Norton only had facilities for the old hearth-brazing methods, all Featherbeds were made at Reynolds Tubes, which guaranteed quality but limited potential output. If in doubt of a Featherbed's date, Reynolds stamped them all with the month and year of manufacture, but using very small stamps, on the edge of one of the headsteady attachment lugs.

The Featherbed was a duplex loop design with a short swinging-arm. The two main loops of tube were welded to the bottom of the headstock. From the headstock they angled outward and ran back horizontally as the tank top rails, with the tank resting on top of them on rubber mountings, secured down its length by a metal top strap. The twin tubes were then bent down to run behind the gearbox, and then bent forward again to pass beneath the box and the engine. Bent upwards once more to form the frame's front downtubes, they were then sprung into position inside the top tube rails, where they were welded to both the rails and the headstock.

This unique crossover bracing arrangement would prove exceptionally resistant to the intense torsional stresses of tarmac racing speeds. A rear sub-frame was at first bolted onto the main loops, and formed the top mounting for the suspension units; for 1955 this became welded-on. Four cross-tubes were welded in to brace the main tubes, as well as support gussets welded to the tube loops by the swinging-arm. Three of the cross-tubes carried steel mounting-plates for the

engine and gearbox, one of them the headsteady; as Rex McCandless put it, "the engine was a very important part of the frame."

The frame was married to a new version of Norton's renowned Roadholder front forks, the broadset, sturdiest telescopics in the industry, and incorporating genuine two-way damping. This version's stanchions were 2 inches shorter than the previous ones, so they were known as "short" Roadholders. They were carried at the relatively steep head angle of 62 degrees, contributing to the excellent high speed handling.

One early Featherbed problem that surfaced was that the headstock arrangement did not provide enough reinforcement when a machine was bumped up over a kerb, so that this simple stress could push

Norton "cigar" silencers, and rear brake with flimsy backplate. Non-standard chromed shrouds on Girling units are a nice, typically café touch.

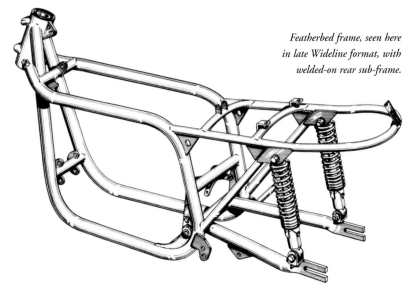

Featherbed frame, seen here in late Wideline format, with welded-on rear sub-frame.

the front forks back. Frame guru Ken Sprayson at Reynolds solved this for the roadsters by adding a gusset at the headstock. But when the twin engine was later deployed to power "desert sleds" racing in the American West, the frames used were to be the old brazed-lug kind from either Norton or AMC, better able to withstand off-road shocks. Featherbeds also featured a less suitable, rather restricted steering lock. On the road, however, the Featherbed was undisputed King. "You steer it with your nose," as one rider put it – just looking at or thinking of a line

Pukka "Norton straight" bars and Slimline tank badge. No rev counter, but in the headlamp shell below the Joe Lucas badge the 150mph speedo discreetly made its point

got you round it, on rails.

Norton twin engine development continued, with the first alloy head fitted in 1955, along with full-width hubs for the 8-inch front, 7-inch rear brakes. The latter would always prove unsatisfactory due to a flimsy back-plate, with this aggravated in 1962 by an upturned cam expander lever (adopted to suit briefly-offered US silencers and then never altered back), which adversely affected the brake's operation. The single leading shoe front could be satisfactory, but tests noted more than one example leaving the factory with oval drums.

From May 1956 the gearbox became the even better AMC version, for in 1953 the Woolwich-based AMC group, manufacturers of AJS and Matchless machines, had taken over Norton. Despite the presence of BSA and Triumph 650s since 1950, both Norton and AMC were cautious about expanding their twins, which for 1956 both went to just 600, the Norton engine being bored and stroked at 68 x 82mm to produce the 596cc Dominator 99.

With slightly higher compression, and the sports Daytona camshaft developed for the races there, the 31bhp 600 was noticeably increased in performance. In fact it was the first production Norton ton-up twin, just scraping in at 101mph, but with 70 in second and 89 in third, and snappy through the gears, with 0-60 coming up in just 7 seconds. It was still a flexible motor, too. Norton handling, race-bred and demonstrably excellent, wet or dry, was always well respected by the leather boys. But the 600 until 1961 was looked on as essentially a touring motor, lacking the T110's performance edge.

They were also still expensive, around 10% more than the Triumph equivalents, and hard to come by. With a workforce of around 500, Bracebridge Street production even in a peak year like 1958 never exceeded 250 machines a week and often fell well below that, so annual output was never more than 9000 at best, including "Light" twins and singles, between a half and a third of Triumph's production. Add in the fact that, thanks to the shortage of cash due to AMC mismanagement, by 1966 some 80% of AMC production, the majority of it by then Nortons, were going to their US distributor Joe Berliner, and it is clear why these excellent motorcycles were always much thinner on the ground in the UK than the popular Triumphs.

The 600 Dominator 99 also had a few problems. Very early on there was trouble with their wire-wound Automotive pistons, until these were altered. More fundamentally, if raced, the crankshaft's 1½-inch diameter crankpins could become overstressed by the extra 10mm or so stroke, and break; this had never happened with the 500. The 99 could be and was ridden hard on the road. My college friend Mike Sewell, who introduced me to Nortons, ran a '56 600 in the early Sixties, and as he put it, with no upper

speed limit and a lot less traffic then, "From my home in Bristol to my digs in Oxford became one long race-track." Mike tuned his early machine with components from the later 650SS, "but when ridden hard it would still gobble up timing side main bearings at a regular rate."

A further problem involved the barrels. The Dominator's weakest point, as tuners found out, was the iron cylinder barrel. In normal trim for road use they were fine, but if over-bored and fitted with high compression pistons, they could split; and the base

1962 650SS with asymmetrical rev counter fitting; twinned instruments as standard only came for 1967. Note inner-tube band wrapped round throttle, a road tester's dodge to get maximum grip and leverage.

650SS's long tank, though narrower than the previous "Wideline's", with 3.6 gallon capacity gave a useful range.

Norton "cigar" silencers still produced a healthy roar, while chromed mudguards offered just the right amount of flash. Alloy wheel rims are non-standard, like the units' chromed upper covers.

returned to Bracebridge Street in 1956, with Doug Hele joining him, and in 1958 Hopwood became MD. For 1957 a new, lighter cast aluminium full-width hub 8-inch front brake was adopted, and judged good. 1958 saw a step back in sports terms, with alternator and coil electrics adopted by the 88 and 99. In our period, with 6-volt alternators and their charging systems far from reliable, sports riders strongly preferred a self-contained magneto for ignition, rather than depending on the state of the battery for starting and running, as you did with coil ignition. They noted that magnetos were used in boats and piston-engined aircraft, where failure could be life-threatening. The 600, even in the coming SS format, never regained a magneto.

To sugar the pill, from May 1958 optional twin carburettors on a suitable splayed manifold were offered. Doug Hele and his colleague Brian Stimson were developing the twins apace, with performance parts tested for hundreds of miles on selected machines, like journalist Bruce Main-Smith's personal Dominator. The 600 twin-carb export-only Nomad "desert sled" also provided feedback. In 1959 larger diameter inlet valves became an option for the 88 and 99. That year AMC twins made the jump to the 650 capacity, but whether due to a Plumstead veto, or prudence, or simply lack of funds, Norton would stay at the 600 stepping stone until 1961 for export, and 1962 for the UK.

For 1960 it was the famous frame that was modified. The existing Featherbed, known retrospectively as the "Wideline", had indeed been 11½ inches wide across, at the rear of the petrol tank and the broad seat nose, which was potentially uncomfortable for the short of stature, and with the bike at rest could make it difficult for them to get their feet flat on the ground. The new "Slimline" version was introduced ostensibly to address this, permitting a narrower seat nose and slimmer 3.6-gallon tank, no longer fastened by a top strap, but secured from below at the front with two inverted bolts with rubber bushes, and held down at the rear by a thick band of rubber.

But the real reason for the Slimline was so that Norton could go down the Triumph route and fit a version of the rear panelling, first seen for 1959 on the unit Jubilee "Light" 250 twin, on the larger-capacity, pre-unit machines, where the results were known as the De-Luxe models. Apart from the appearance and some impracticality – a luggage rack could not be fitted, and the panelling had to come off to get at the carb – the format restricted the De-Luxe twins to a single carburettor. Norton would abandon the big twin's panelling relatively quickly, in 1963 – but not quickly enough to stop me later getting lumbered

flange of the barrel could break off alarmingly easily. Boring out beyond + 0.040 was not advisable. (This was interesting in the light of a reader's letter to Motorcycle News. Though the 650 would be catalogued with the same bore as the 600, after the reader's 600 had been bored out to +0.040, no suitable pistons could be found – until he tried a standard 650 piston which fitted the over-bore perfectly. With his racing 650 Syd Lawton had found that early piston-to-barrel clearance was very tight, enough to cause seizure; but after honing out his barrel to +0.050, he used it for three trouble-free racing seasons. Had the factory quietly done the same with the 650 road bikes?)

Development continued. Bert Hopwood had

with an 88 De-Luxe, becoming another victim of the scarcity of Norton twins in the UK.

The Slimline was achieved by bending the tubes differently just above the rear gusset, kinking the back of the main loop inwards, with the tubes at the front bent a little more to match. With "tea-cup handle" loops and cantilever brackets on the rear frame for mounting the panels, there was some loss of triangulation. The rear units were shortened by just under an inch, and the Slimline's steering head angle was altered by a couple of degrees. (Interestingly however, Bill Cakebread in his memoir *Motorcycle Apprentice*, about his time at Plumstead, recalled how during his period in the Drawing Office he was tasked with curing the Slimline Featherbed-framed models' habit of denting their front mudguards on the frame when the forks were on full compression. In the course of this he discovered that the frame's headstock tube was still welded at the former Wideline's angle! He guessed that this might have been due to a draughtsman's error, drawing retrospectively from a prototype. Current Norton expert Les Emery of Fairspares confirmed both the suspect head angle and the mudguard-fouling problem with Nortons from this period.)

In the cafes the Wideline was preferred because it looked more like a Manx racer and provided a marginally better basis for a Triton. Some have felt that the Slimline caused a slight reduction in Norton handling excellence, possibly because the narrower spread of the top rails meant less resistance to torsional forces when cornering hard. If this was the case it only applied for racing, as there was never a question mark over the Slimline for fast road use, including on the 650SS. The man at the sharp end of production racing, Syd Lawton, believed that any handling problem was more likely to be due, from 1958 on, to the weight of the "alternator being slung on the end of the crank, and of the much bigger clutches." His effective solution on the "Lawton Norton" 650 was to rebuild both wheels with their rims pulled fractionally to the left.

For the 88 and 99 1960 had seen larger inlet valves adopted as standard, and together with a new higher-lift camshaft this hoisted the 99's output to a claimed 34bhp. The 600 acquired more finning on the cylinder block, and in the gearbox of both twins a previous irritating gap between third and top was closed up. "Norton straights" were offered, characteristic short, flat handlebars bent slightly rearwards to provide a great compromise riding position for fast work and touring.

Meanwhile Hele and Stimson had been working on a pure track 500 twin, originally conceived to contest Daytona, and then developed as a successor to the ohc singles. 35lbs lighter than an 88, it was entered in 1961's Senior TT. A young Mike Hailwood won the race on a Bill Lacey-tuned Manx, beating Hocking's MV-Four in a last burst of black and silver racing glory. But sensationally the 54bhp Domiracer came third, with a best lap of 100.36mph, not to be equalled by a pushrod twin until 1969 (and then it was a 750).

Racer and Norton specialist Paul Dunstall, who would take over the Domiracer and all its spares, confirmed that while it externally resembled an 88, "I don't think one bolt or casting was the same." It featured needle-roller bearing camshafts with oil-feed lobes, forged two-ring pistons, heavier duty con rods, crankshaft and main bearings, along with chrome-alloy barrels, and cylinder heads with squish-bands and downdraught twin carbs. Some of these developments fed into the new 650, which, after initial development assistance from US importer Joe Berliner, was released for export only in 1961. Its Manxman name reflected the Island glory, and its styling American tastes, with a smaller pear-shaped gas tank, high-rise pullback handlebars, a 4.00 x 18-inch rear wheel, a light metallic blue paint job and a red seat.

Meanwhile, in the UK for April 1961, the SS variants of the 88 and 99 were released. For them twin carbs on splayed manifolds were standard, with inlet ports opened out and, along with the combustion chambers, polished. Compression was raised. The Daytona cam and its flat-based cam followers as found on the Manxman, plus two-rate valve springs, extra

650SS ton-plus performance deserves this non-standard twin leading shoe front brake from early 750 Commando.

Bert Hopwood (left) introduces the American Ambassador to Norton's first 650, the 1961 US export-only Manxman.

Hopwood accumulated for the purpose, among other things, of a move to new premises where production could be increased, had been removed in 1960 by a peremptory demand from Plumstead for a cheque for a quarter of a million pounds to meet "a minor cash crisis." Attempts by shareholders to oust the inefficient top management had failed in 1961, and by 1962 when they succeeded, the group financial situation was so bad that Norton had to close up in Birmingham, and production was moved down to South East London.

DOMINATION PLUS DECLINE

Against this looming background the 650SS was launched in the UK for the 1962 model year, and as noted, it was an instant hit. Hele had significantly strengthened the motor: as Dunstall put it, "The reliability we'd been losing on the 600 came back with the 650." Hele had also restored the engine's flexibility and unfussiness, with the longer 89mm stroke contributing. Testers admired the 650's behaviour in traffic, finding "a sporting top end without the bad manners associated with such urge at low speeds."

The urge itself derived from a combination of the sound basic design and Hele's development; as Syd Lawton said, Hele "regarded production racing as a means of improving the breed." The redesigned downdraught twin-carb cylinder head, first seen on the Domiracer, lay at the heart of this. While the 500 88SS was now fitted with it, the 99SS was not (a final strike, as the 600 was in its last season). There was a 20-degree downdraught angle for the twin 1 1/16-inch 389 Monoblocs, the right-hand one with a chopped-off float bowl. With this head, Hele had widened the rather narrow inlet port centres, and the inlet passage in the 650 head was sleeved down from 1 1/8 inch to 1 1/16 inch with steel inserts, something which again had been found to increase mid-range power and response. As on Bonnevilles from late 1960, there was a balance pipe between the Norton's twin induction tracts to help smooth running at lower speeds.

Hele had also widened the exhaust ports, which enabled them to be shortened and therefore collect less heat. The head featured larger inlet valves and multi-rate valve springs. The pushrods were the barrel-shaped type, and the camshaft the Daytona. As Dunstall observed, "The sound cylinder head design is the key…The twin carb head is easily the biggest single improvement you can make" [to a Dominator]. The Norton's became recognised as the best-breathing cylinder head in the industry.

The engine's extra strength derived principally from a revised crankshaft, with the crankcases redesigned to suit. It featured larger big end journals

strong clutch springs and hollow, barrel-shaped alloy pushrods, all resulted in a claimed output for the 99SS of 44bhp at 6750rpm. The 500 88SS, but not the 99SS (another strike against it) had a Lucas K2FC magneto for ignition, with a lower-output alternator. Ball-ended control levers, a racing requirement, were standard, with options including rear-sets and a rev counter (driven via a boss on the timing cover and mounted on a bracket next to the headlamp shell), as well as a siamesed exhaust system.

Hard-riding tester and racer Vic Willoughby for *The Motor Cycle* found the siamesed system made an appreciable difference to power on the test 99SS, which he also found had much quicker throttle response than the standard 99. He saw an impressive 108mph at the top end, as well as prolonged cruising at 90mph. But as would also be the case on the 88SS, he noted that high-speed acceleration was more marked than torque at lower speeds, with a bit less punch below 4500rpm. The price of the top speed had been some peakiness, as well as increased vibration plus increased thirst, with overall mpg in the mid-40s.

The SS debut had sadly coincided with Bert Hopwood's departure for better prospects at Triumph; Hele would join him 18 months later in August 1962. By that time the closure of Bracebridge Street had been announced. Norton's relationship with their parent AMC group had always been fraught, with what Hopwood characterized as "great jealousy at Woolwich of any Norton successes." All profit

(1¾ inch diameter against the previous 1½ inch), and a wider, heavier flywheel. As Hele himself remarked with typical understatement, "We were quite pleased with the 650SS. We fitted it with a big flywheel and the vibration level was acceptable," and tests confirmed that the 650's vibration was reasonable. 8.9:1 compression pistons with solid skirts were used, featuring a Twiflex oil control ring, an unusual type of scraper ring comprising two small rings located on each side of the steeped portion of the expander ring.

The engine breather was revised, becoming of the rotary timed type, with surplus oil mist from it helping to lubricate the rear chain. To cope with the extra power, an extra (5th) plate was fitted in the clutch. The 650SS was fitted with the same magneto and RM19 alternator as the 88SS. Options included the 4.00 x 18 rear wheel and the siamesed exhaust system, but the latter was rarely specified as the factory advised that on the 650 it had been found to inhibit acceleration, though not top speed.

Tests confirmed the performance and the tractability ("Approaches two miles a minute yet eats out of your hand"). In addition there was good (front) braking (28½ft from 30mph), bearable shakes, and fair economy (50mpg overall). And of course, there was the superior handling and roadholding, in the wet or the dry. Production racing success confirmed it too. Lawton's riders Phil Read/Brian Setchell were outright winners of both the 1962 BMCRC Silverstone 1000 kms race and the Thruxton 500. They won Thruxton again in 1963, and once more, with Setchell/Derek Woodman, for 1964. Lawton confirmed that, apart from fitting a home-brewed Manx-derived close-ratio gearbox, "we didn't tune for extra power and perform-ance." The stock 650SS was that good. After years living in the shadow of the charismatic Triumphs, the unassuming, classically handsome Norton twin had come into its own.

Hele had seen the 650 to fruition before leaving. He had also laid out, at Berliner's request, a soft-tuned, torquey 750 version, the Atlas, the aim being to satisfy American requests for a twin that could accelerate from 20mph to 100 in top gear. Released for 1962 in the US and from February 1964 in the UK, the Atlas was claimed to equal the 650's power at 49bhp, though in private AMC's chief designer Jack Williams claimed that the true figure on the early soft-tuned versions was 44bhp. After Doug Hele's strict guidelines that the 7.5:1 compression and tune should never be raised any further were ignored by Plumstead, the Atlas quickly gained both more power and a (justified) reputation for punishing vibration; although developed still further, the 750 would power the Commando which carried

Norton Dominator 650
650 c.c. Vertical Twin

SPORTS

Specially designed for the rider who wants extra performance, these really powerful machines have been produced to give, not only high performance but also the highest degree of safety. For high speed cruising and motor-way travel, or production machine racing, these Sports Specials are the tops.

ENGINE. 647 c.c. O.H.V. vertical twin with basic specification similar to the 650 c.c. machines but with twin carburettors incorporating special balance system in induction tracts to facilitate low speed running. Magneto ignition with automatic advance and retard mecha-nism. Maximum power is developed at 6,800 r.p.m. giving 49 b.h.p.
GEARBOX. 4 speed positive foot change with heavy duty, multi-plate clutch as fitted to all 650 c.c. machines.
FORKS. "Roadholder" forks; straight handlebars and racing-type ball ended levers.
FRAME. Racebred "Featherbed" frame, famous for its safe road-holding qualities and extreme rigidity.
BRAKES. Front, 8" × 1¼". Rear, 7" × 1¼". Very powerful, non-fade.
LIGHTING. Crankshaft mounted alternator for lighting only: 13 A.H. battery; powerful, adjustable, 8" headlamp with 150 m.p.h. speedometer and lighting switch in headlamp shell. Combined rear/stop lamp with built-in reflector.
TYRES. Avon 3.00 × 19 front, 3.50 × 19 G.P. rear tyre. Q.D. rear wheel.
OPTIONAL EQUIPMENT. 2 into 1 exhaust pipes.
OPTIONAL EXTRAS. Folding kick start. Rev. counter. Chrome guards. Fully enclosed rear chain case.
COLOUR FINISH. All black with silver tank.

the Norton story into the mid-1970s.

Only five Norton workers had made the trip down to London in February 1963 and only one of them, the trouble-shooting engineer John Hudson, stuck it out there. Norton production for 1963, as Plumstead got to grips with quirky or damaged Bracebridge Street machinery, was a mere 2500, including perhaps 1000 "Light" twins. From then on no more than 4000 Nortons a year, all models included, would be made before AMC's collapse into Receivership in August 1966, the takeover by Dennis Poore to form Norton-Villiers, and the final end of production at Plumstead in 1969.

So no more than a few thousand of the peerless 650SS were made, and many of those went to America before their production ceased at the end of the 1968 model year, with a coda of the single-carb 650 Mercury for the following year. By then the Rocker era was fading into memory, and because the 650SS came late to the café scene a real opportunity had been missed. Yet its popularity among British riders (that

New for 1962, with the 650SS it was any colour you liked as long as it was silver.

650SS dominated Production racing from 1962 to 1964.

Motorcycle News vote), and the undoubted respect, if not quite affection, which it inspired among the leather boys, suggests that it could have sold a lot more despite the declining market and its uncompetitive price.

Like any motorcycle, the 650SS had its weak points. At first the con rods occasionally proved occasionally prone to fracture until they were strengthened in mid-1965. The alloy heads meant that the threaded rings retaining the exhaust pipes in it were vulnerable to cross-threading and to wear from vibration from then on. The downdraught carburettors meant were always prone to flooding, needed little or no carb tickling, and with the machine at rest the petrol tap

Tom Phillis aboard the 500 Domiracer, storming to third place in the 1961 Senior TT and setting long-standing 100mph-plus class lap record.

always had to be turned off. If it was not, as well as flooding the combustion chambers, petrol would flow down past the inlet valve and piston rings, wash the bores, and dilute the oil in the crankcase. In addition, sometimes the chopped-float twin carbs could suffer from fuel starvation.

Development after the move south was sporadic, and not always helpful. Plumstead's development chief, the cautious Charles Udall, decided that the 650 and Atlas main bearing clearances were too generous and should alter to be a "crunch fit", much tighter on the shaft. John Hudson, appalled, said "They bashed them on in the end." The reduced clearance on the new bearings between the internal elements of balls and rollers and the steel track did not allow for expansion of the shaft, and this caused bearing failures until it was sorted out.

In 1964 the electrics changed to 12 volts, and the Roadholder forks' centres increased from 7-inch to 7⅜-inch to take wider tyres for America, with the new ones identifiable by the presence of a steering lock. Late 1965 saw the problem with the head-to-barrel spigot tackled, by removing both the spigot and the matching recesses in the head, which also permitted more support for the outer ends of the rocker spindles to be provided in the cylinder head casting. The gasket at first became copper-asbestos, but changed to a black Hallite one with a flame ring, as without the spigot to protect it from the flame the tiny section of copper remaining in the head-bolts soon burnt away.

In 1966 the lubrication system was overhauled, in John Hudson's view unnecessarily, with a 6-start oil pump doubling the delivery, enlarged internal oilways, and pressure feed to the rockers, which became plain rather than scrolled as previously, and ¼ inch narrower. As mentioned, the con rods had been strengthened, and mid-year the carburettors became handed, each with its own float chamber. 1967 saw, too late for most café racers, a paired speedo and rev counter as standard, mounted on a chrome bracket. The Monobloc carburettors changed to Concentrics, and late in the year the electrics became alternator and coil. In 1968 the seat gained a rear hump, and with the 750 Commando coming on stream 650SS production ceased in February.

I was lucky enough to own a three-year-old 1966 650SS as my sole transport for three years and rode it far and wide, with regular trips back and forward on fast A-roads from London to Norfolk, plus jaunts to Ireland, France, Spain, and all round Morocco. Nothing broke. The handling was so good you forgot about it, and the bike's stability was particularly appreciated in Norfolk's wet and sometimes icy winter conditions. It was not a comfortable machine, with the firm transmission and suspension and an un-luxurious seat, and it was noisy mechanically in a tappety way. It was good two-up with plenty of low-down power, though on long runs the passenger suffered just as the rider did. But I didn't ride it like a Rocker, rarely exceeding 75mph, where the vibration got noticeable. The downdraught carburettor complications were irritating, and though with the magneto it was always a reliable starter – if not an easy one with the relatively high compression – more than once I had to bump-start it due to my own folly in letting it get flooded. It was like a gruff male companion, good-looking in an understated way, utterly reliable, only with emotional input surplus to requirement.

SS downdraught twin carbs could be a pain, but were an important part of the Norton's performance package. AMC/Norton gearbox was the best.

TECHNICAL SPECIFICATIONS:
1958 NORTON 650SS

Capacity	647cc
Bore	68mm
Stroke	89mm
Compression	8.9:1
Power output	49bhp@6800rpm
Electrical system	6 volt
Ignition	Magneto
Generator	Alternator
Wheels and tyres	F: 3.00x19. R: 3.50x19
Brakes	F: 8-inch. R: 7-inch
Weight (dry)	398lbs
Max speed	111.9mph

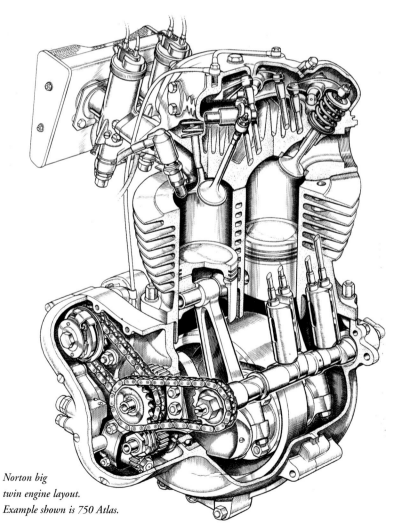

Norton big twin engine layout. Example shown is 750 Atlas.

CHAPTER 8:
AJS/MATCHLESS MODEL 31CSR/G12CSR

"The secret with CSRs seemed to be putting them together properly. Another guy had one of the '62 TT Marshal's Matchless twins, with all the speed equipment – but it never went well. One night though, it was finally going really right, and he decided to do a run past Johnson's. But his overtrousers were bungied to the back of his seat, and they'd flapped loose and got tangled in the rear wheel. It put him off on the A20 at over a hundred. He was all right. But he was a bit sick about the bike."

Former AMC worker Harry Winch

A symphony of polished alloy (those mudguards) and chrome, the ton-plus '63 CSR for a while was a force to be reckoned with.

AMC, with their core AJS and Matchless marques made in East London at Plumstead, south of the Woolwich ferry, were by 1960 the oldest continuous British motorcycle manufacturers. But they had lost their way, both financially and in terms of the brand.

They had an impeccable sporting pedigree, which should have appealed to the lads. One of the founder's sons, Charlie Collier, had won the singles class of the first ever TT on a Matchless, and throughout the Fifties the track ohc single 350 AJS 7R "Boy Racer", and later the 500 Matchless G50, were staples of

Clubman competition, even after works racing had ceased in 1956. But these pure ohc racers cost over £100 more than the top twins and Gold Stars, and had little appeal for the café crowd. And little of the racing glamour seemed to rub off onto their own twin-cylinder roadsters in the Fifties, and despite a racing version of the G9 500, the G45, being available from 1952 to 1958, it never thrived.

The start of the group's decline has generally been pinpointed to the death of the last Collier brother, Charlie, in 1954. The goodwill generated by the early adoption of BMW-derived "Teledraulic" front forks ahead of other British manufacturers, as found on the wartime "Forces' Favourite" Matchless G3L single, would be dissipated by short-sighted leadership from '54 on under Donald Heather. "For management it was all about money," said ex-AMC tester Harry Winch. AJS and Matchless always appealed to an older rider with their "Heavyweight" big singles, and in the Fifties they developed by agonisingly tiny increments with minor, inexpensive changes each year, a storeman's and restorer's nightmare, rather than with any genuinely new direction aimed at the rising generation, other than the unsuccessful "Lightweight" (sic) singles. The rather narrow Teledraulic forks limited

the tyre size, and the brakes remained an inadequate 7-inch single leading shoe front and rear to the end – both issues where money could, and should, have been spent.

Eventual efforts to appeal to the youth and the café crowd would often be ill-judged and inappropriate – the two-tone colour schemes for 1960, and the "knee-knocker" or "Flintstone Special" outsize metal tank badges for 1962, the same year all models received gratuitous names. The G12CSR became the Monarch, while the AJS Model 31CSR was more memorably the Hurricane (ten years before the name would go on the factory-custom Triumph triple). No one paid any attention.

None of it was wanted or needed for 650 machines which had initially suffered a fundamental problem when pushed hard – their crankshafts could break, usually near the drive-side bobweight. There were also problems with rapid camshaft wear, plus piston, barrel, gudgeon pin and blowing head gasket trouble, as well as harsh, tank-splitting vibration. But if the standard 650 model looked much like just another Triumph or BSA twin, elements of the CSR version's styling were appreciated by the leather boys, and towards the finish of the pure AMC line, for '62 and

Very, very British. This was AJS/Matchless twins' last year in thoroughbred form.

"Knee-knocker" tank badges had been suggested by Joe Berliner, AMC's importer in the USA.

name in America, the G50 ohc 500 single came out as a Matchless.

The quality of Plumstead's fine finish and of its engineering was respected. More than most, tooling was kept up to date, with £1,000,000 spent re-tooling in the Fifties, so that by mid-decade their heat treatment and inspection equipment was among the most modern in Europe, with contract work undertaken for Ford across the Thames at Dagenham, and for Rolls-Royce. But too much time and money had gone into the racing effort, and into follies like their own Piatti-designed two-stroke engine, plus expensive planning for an aborted move to the Isle of Sheppey, while they were effectively failing to get into the big bike market until 1959.

SOMETHING DIFFERENT

AMC had entered the twin market for 1949, with a 498cc model, the G9/Model 20, featuring swinging-arm suspension from the start when only Royal Enfield were doing likewise. Designer Phil Walker had made his engine strikingly different, with an alloy cylinder head, years before most others; with separate barrels under the common head, which again only Royal Enfield had tried (and without the latter's "shuffling" problems); and with the crankshaft running, uniquely, on three main bearings. The intention was to stop the crankshaft acting as a skipping-rope between the conventional bearing-at-each-end. But firstly, a degree of crank flexing may actually have had the effect of absorbing vibration for the rider.

And secondly, the AMC twin's middle main bearing, a split shell like a big end, was sandwiched between twin, full disc internal flywheels. The bearing was carried on a detachable location web, and not very rigidly located by the web's six puny ¼-inch anchor studs. So it may actually not have been located securely enough to stop the vibes. The setting of the centre web was considered the crucial art in assembling an AMC twin engine, as it had to be dowelled to the crankcase in a particular manner developed for the G45 racer; so this was not a feature friendly to home rebuilders. Journalist Bruce Main-Smith (BMS), who rode a lot of AMC twins, in the end considered that their unusual layout seemed to give no worthwhile advantage.

With bobweights located at the crankshaft's outer ends, and gear drive for the twin camshafts and for the magneto, the AMC 500 did not experience the shakes which came with later, larger capacities. It was exceptionally carefully built, with the flywheels balanced, and with them a pair of con rods made and marked together, being weighed to within 10g of each other, and the same thing done with a pair of pistons. All

'63, the 650CSR became quite a formidable tool, as things sometimes do just before the end. However, as ex-Rocker and AMC Hybrid expert Paul Morin put it, "In the early days"(around 1962) "the CSR 650s were respected, but not in the later" ('64-on) "period – they were too slow in comparison with the Bonnie."

AJS and Matchless machines were near-identical after 1952, when the Matchless's magneto had moved from behind the cylinder to in front of it, like the Ajay's. But they were still made, styled and marketed separately, in an expensive sop to marque loyalty. On the twins, the only major differences were that the AJS timing cover featured twin bulges for the engine's unusual twin oil pumps, where the Matchless cover was smooth; and the Matchless sported megaphone silencers against the AJS's more conventional type, with a tail-pipe exiting at the top. The characteristic AJS finish was gold-lined black, or if a colour was involved, blue, while the Matchless featured a touch of red. AJS was ostensibly the competition marque, yet the more sporting of the first 500 twins was the Matchless G9 Super Clubman with its less restricted "squashed megaphone" silencers at first, and after it was realised that Matchless was the better-known

Monarch of all he surveys,
aboard this King of Bling,
the '63 Matchless 650CSR.

this may well have contributed to the fact that the 500 twins were said to have been produced at a loss from Day One!

At £217 in 1949, they cost 10% more than a Triumph Tiger 100 and nearly £40 more than a Speed Twin. So they were always the quality option, and very reliable and durable indeed. They were not that numerous either, as peak Plumstead production was 80 machines a day in the mid-Fifties, and never exceeded 15,000 a year, with much going for export. Pleasant as they were to ride, top speeds in the high 80s were unexceptional. The handling was fine for every day, but if pushed, thanks to AMC's proprietary "Jampot" rear units, in the words of racer Mike Apted, it was "like a little puppy dog – it was always wagging its tail." Nevertheless works off-road ace Hugh Viney took Gold at the ISDT on a Model 20 for three years running from 1950, his machines featuring the first siamesed exhausts for these models.

The high-speed handling began to improve with the adoption in 1957 of Girling rear units, though until 1963 these featured unique clevis (stirrup-shaped) lower mountings to suit the AMC spring frame. Meanwhile 1956 had seen the arrival of the G11/Model 30 592cc twin, achieved by boring out the G9's 66mm to 72mm, but retaining its 72.8 stroke. This was the limit for over-boring – a small

batch of AMC's own 750 twins built in 1962 would prove unviable due to insufficient meat at the cylinder head joint. 600cc was the limit and the only way was up, with a new crank to create the 650's longer stroke being an expensive proposition for the company.

So for three years they stuck with just the 600. Some felt it was an ideal compromise between the 500's limited soft power and the 650's harshness, and the point was certainly made that in CSR form it could be a ton-plus machine. *Motor Cycle* journalist and racer Vic Willoughby early in 1958 rode a G11CSR to MIRA, and with just a larger main jet in the carburettor, during the lunch hour when there was no "traffic", circulated the 2.8mile track at an average of just over 103mph – and then rode it back from Warwickshire to London.

This had been a breakthrough in more than one way, as uniquely there was a veto on Press testing of AJS/Matchless machinery. Apparently this was because boss Donald Heather had once been on the staff of *Motor Cycling* but had fallen out with his superiors and been asked to leave, and still had a chip on his shoulder about it. Sales Director and ex-racer Jock West justified the ban by saying the company was selling everything it produced anyway, but this was short-sighted as it meant AMC riders in clubs and cafés could not bandy statistics like the fans of other

No race kit, so simply a single large (and easy to live with) Monobloc carb. Note cooling fins emerging from beneath the exhaust ports for '60-on cylinder head.

CSR's siamesed exhaust system, seen here in early form on 600cc G11CSR.

marques; and in the Sixties the sales situation deteriorated to the point that the factory would remove the year of manufacture previously featured as part of the engine number so that unsold stock could not be identified as such the following year.

The 600 had virtues. They were relatively oil-tight, with the only habitual leak being at the base of the barrels. For 1958 an excellent and handsome alloy chaincase had come, along with selective adoption in the range of alternator electrics, to replace the previous leak-prone pressed-steel cover, although none of the twins' electrics would change till the following year; and the CSRs would always retain their magneto for ignition, with manual advance/retard control. In addition the fine AMC gearbox had been adopted for 1957, though for the twins its ratios included an annoyingly wide gap between third and top. Clutch slip could also be a habitual problem if the chaincase oil level was too high.

The standard G11 may have been mild, but the CSR versions, as Willoughby's exploit had proved, were not. With 8.5:1 compression and modified inlet ports and chambers (modified by Willoughby in his capacity as part-time development engineer), the power was said to be up from the standard model's 33bhp to 38.5. Developed from the US export CS (Convertible Scrambler), and featuring a scrambles frame similar to the off-road singles', with increased ground clearance, a thicker front downtube, and its rear loop in one piece rather than the standard two bottom rails running under the engine, this model began to accumulate style points that would appeal to the ton-up crew. It featured an optional chrome-panelled petrol tank, a QD headlamp shell, a slim, short twinseat, a fashionable siamesed exhaust running to the right into an AJS-type silencer whether or not it was badged a Matchless, and the much-envied alloy racing mudguards, not too effective against British weather but definitely looking the business.

Only a few 600 CSRs were released, and factory tester Harry Winch saw this as evidence of the management's "inability to listen. From 1958 to 1962," he said, "was the true age of the coffee bar cowboy, with the Bonneville and Super Rocket all selling well. That was when the CSR was needed – that basic look was nice. And it had already been about, from the early Fifties – in the shape of our ISDT twins. Instruments on brackets, siamesed exhausts, upswept pipes, it was basically the look of the CSR." But though an export-oriented, street scrambler version of the 650, the G12/Model 31CSR, was available in the UK from 1959, "they didn't come out with the first [twin carb] race-kit CSRs until

1962. Too late. It was very short-sighted."

The G11CSR/Model 30CSR were released in the UK, catalogued as the Sports Twin, in January 1958, and doomed to be a short-lived, rare model, as the 650 was already being manufactured, that year for US export only. What did CSR stand for? Bruce Main-Smith was told "Competition Springer Racing", but when he pointed out that "Springer" was illogical since they hadn't produced an unsprung model for several years, this was modified to "Competition Sports Roadster". But the lads already knew it stood for "Coffee Shop Racer"… With the 650 imminent, not many 600 CSRs were made, and some of those were converted to 650s at the factory. With the higher compression, the one I test-rode, while it performed well, did so in a nervy, unrelaxed fashion, a world away from the extremely likeable (but slower) standard 500 twin.

BIGGER BANG

The 650 in the UK from 1959, with its new long-stroke (79.3mm) crank giving 646cc, was, in a word, beefier. But it got off to a rocky start. Crankshafts did break, and word of this spread, as did, even without road tests until 1961, knowledge of the harsh vibration, particularly for the 8.5:1 compression CSRs. Vic Willoughby was disappointed, after the quick G11CSR, with his 1959 G12 staff bike, its vibration severe enough to split the petrol tank and loosen off well-tightened nuts, plus the fact that the shakes were worst at his habitual cruising speed of 90 mph.

Bruce Main-Smith got a '59 G12CSR for his personal mount, and after 32,000 miles later rated it his "worst bike ever" – it split no less than 15 petrol tanks with its vibration; though this might partially have been due to that year's 4¼-gallon tanks, with their seam now on the top centre line. The Teledraulics he felt were showing their age and chattering at speed, so he modified their internals with cut-down dampers from Girling which gave double rebound damping, and would be used (unofficially) on later racers at Thruxton. But he acknowledged the bike as comfortable, including for the passenger, a good starter with a lovely exhaust note, with excellent handling – and said it vibrated less than his (unit construction) Triumph 650 Saint which followed it.

The cracked cranks, however, could not be ignored, although with the standard 650 adopting a crankshaft-mounted RM15 alternator for all its electrics, and the breakages coming on the drive side where the alternator was mounted, that may have been a factor as Syd Lawton suggested. AMC went to their friends at Ford for advice, and progressively from 1960 the crankshaft material was changed. Contrary

AMC twin engine's look was very distinctive, with '60-on alloy head a big step forward in performance terms.

Vic Willoughby on 1958 G11CSR circulating MIRA fast. He would cover just over 103 miles in an hour.

Derided at the time, defiantly loud and proud '62-on zinc alloy tank badges play well with chrome tank.

Plumstead's original brand – which five years later would be no more.

to accepted wisdom, and as confirmed by Jock West, the material had been nodular iron from the start. But the particles of the earlier type had an irregular physical structure, and this irregular pattern could cause weakness at stress points, particularly on alternator cranks. The later spheroidal graphite nodular iron type avoided this. There was no sharply defined changeover to the new cranks; commencing in 1960, they were made in batches of 20 to 40 at a time (Plumstead lacked a forge of its own so the cranks were bought in), and supplied first to production racers, the police's machines, and favoured customers, until nothing but the new ones were being fitted for the 1962 model year.

Meanwhile two major developments had come for 1960. The engine gained a redesigned cylinder head from Jack Williams, former racer, member of the prestigious Institute of Mechanical Engineers via a thesis on engine breathing and gas flow, and the chief of the AMC Race Shop (as well as father of future Norton racer and designer Peter Williams). Likeable Jack, as BMS put it, "in spare moments" from designing and developing the 7R and G50 "had a look at the twins." Works racer Alan Shepherd who co-developed the G50 called Williams "a top-line engineer who wasn't really given a chance. They were always short of money and Jack performed miracles on a shoe-string budget." As well as the 2.5bhp extra he had found that the siamesed exhaust gave the twins, he told BMS

"Knee-knocker" badges and lightning flash on new-for-'63 petrol tank, in practice worked well visually.

that with the 650's head he had gone for a spread of power rather than straight top speed – "Roadster or racer," said Williams, "I would always trade 2bhp off the top of the power curve for 1 at the bottom. I like my power curves really fat in the middle." AMC were still not releasing power output figures, but Williams would tell BMS that the 650CSR was good for 47.5bhp, while Club racer Bob Doughty had been told that the rare Thruxton 650 he bought in 1960 put out 46bhp at 6200rpm.

The new head, still in alloy, featured a recess round the edge to take the top spigot of the 8-fin barrel. The spigot was now machined thicker than previously, to prevent a mismatch of the new head and old barrels. At the bottom of the barrels, a ridged spigot featured rather than the previous banded one. The head was now held down by ⅜-inch bolts to help cope with CSR's 8.5:1 c.r. (the bolts would change to ⁷⁄₁₆-inch for 1963). It featured additional finning, including three new transverse cooling fins under each exhaust port, which were a sure external identifier of the new head.

Internally the shape of the combustion chamber became hemispherical, and the position of the valves was altered. The valve included angles were reduced to 40 degrees, with arcuate inlet tracts imparting swirl to the incoming mixture, and with the valve stem and the protruding portion of the guide now at one side of the inlet tract, offering less resistance to gas flow. To marry with the new head, the pistons changed

104mph motorcycle deserved better than a 7-inch single leading shoe front brake; though there were few complaints at the time.

Thoughtful rider touch was built-in Tommy bar to assist rear wheel removal.

completely from the previous high-domed type to ones with flatter tops to suit the new shallower combustion chambers. Valve timing was altered, two-rate valve springs fitted, and the stud spacing for the separate manifolds and on the head meant the manifolds were not interchangeable with the previous ones. Externally there were bigger lugs at the front of the head for attachment of the cylinder headsteady.

With a single Amal Monobloc 389 carburettor, like the tourers but featuring a larger main jet, in combination with the exhaust camshaft introduced for all 650s for 1959, plus a new inlet camshaft, this free-breathing head transformed the 650CSR engine into a zestful accelerator with a top speed comfortably over the ton at around 104-105mph, yet retaining good town manners (though you didn't want to drop much below 35mph in top), helped by intelligent use of the magneto's manual advance/retard lever. BMS felt Williams had taken the design to its tuning limit, as evidenced by the

Flip-up tail to rear chainguard was a stylish AMC touch.

1961 Matchless G12CSR, with short seat, siamezed exhaust, detachable chrome tank panels, and alloy mudguards, the rear one with open-mounted tail-light.

AJS-style silencers for both marques' CSRs, whether with more common siamesed exhausts or not – you could order either. Girling units abandoned their clevis lower mount that year. Perky tilt to chainguard tail was a nice Plumstead styling touch.

necessity of using 100 octane "Premium" fuel.

The second major innovation for 1960 was the adoption, in the same year as Triumph, of a twin downtube frame for the twins and Heavyweight singles; in fact it had originated after some frame breakages on G3 350 singles on the rocky trails of Cyprus. With a slightly steeper steering head angle, it improved twin handling perceptibly, though it was heavier than the previous chassis, and still constructed by the old, time-consuming brazed lug methods. On it the petrol tank mounting became 3-point, and for

1963, and Paddy Driver on Matchless 650CSR leads Phil Read on Norton 650SS at BRMCC Silverstone 1,000 km race. Driver went on to win.

1962 there came new soft rubber tank mountings to help fight the splitting tanks. Unpopular smaller scooter-type batteries were fitted with the new frame until 1962.

The frame was quite tall, with a high centre of gravity, and needed some conscious effort cornering, but could be heeled over hard, held the road well and steered excellently. BMS considered it second only to the Featherbed. The only qualification was a vestigial reminder of the earlier tail-wagging tendency. *Motor Cycling's* Editor had persuaded Heather to allow road-testing of AMC machines again, as long as the format was altered to de-emphasise top speed, and no power output figures were given. A subsequent test noted that an AJS 650CSR exhibited "some mild weaving" of the rear end on bumpy 70mph bends, but discounted it; and having experienced it myself at 70 on a particularly well-restored and set-up '63 CSR, I can confirm it was completely controllable and not at all alarming.

Until 1961 the CSR version of the duplex chassis had a different rear frame, without pillion footrest mountings. The siamesed exhaust system, which had its run altered and its mounting system modified for 1961, provided very good ground clearance in contrast to the silencer-scraping standard G12/Model 31, and both centre- and side-stands were exceptionally well tucked in, the penalty being inaccessibility. CSR twins could be ordered with or without the siamesed exhaust.

Other CSR distinctions were a dry weight some 15lbs lighter than the stock 650s, at an eye-catching

381lbs. The 4.5-pint oil tank, like the standard model's one, was double-skinned to protect the rider's leg from heat, a mute indication of the twin's hot running, but the CSR's also featured internal baffles, which helped prevent internal pressure build-up. In the CSR's Teledraulics, the fork springs were stronger.

Downsides included the somewhat harsh power delivery, and the frame's potentially uncomfortable tallness, accentuated by a thin, flat, short dualseat, which was only satisfactorily modified for 1963. The seat then became narrower at the rear end and had its depth reduced at the front, and in combination with a revised petrol tank with no centre seam and with new rear recesses carrying thin rubber knee-grips, although the catalogued seat height remained the same, the riding position became lower and more comfortable (though CSRs did not adopt the standard models' solution for 1963, 18-inch wheels). The only real qualification was that a combination of the frame's good steering lock and the '62-on optional short, down-turned handlebar, could cause painfully-trapped thumbs between the bars and the tank.

Meanwhile the better-handling and more powerful 650CSRs had the honour of being chosen by the hard-riding Isle of Man TT Marshals. More proof of their competitiveness came in 1960 at Thruxton. After Hailwood's 1958 Triumph victory, 1959 saw the overall win go to a BMW R69! This would never do, and the following year all four categories in the race were won by British bikes. Dealers Monty and Ward had entered two AJS Model 31CSRs, which they got from the factory but which were said not to be "special", a claim

reinforced by the facts that a) Geoff Monty sold them on after the race, and b) the machine of Alan Shepherd/Michael O'Rourke retired with a broken crankshaft, so evidently they weren't among the favoured few getting the improved nodular ones.

That left Don Chapman/Ron Langston, the latter a Gloucestershire farmer and seriously talented all-rounder, successful at trials and scrambles as well as on tarmac. Langston had a phlegmatic approach to endurance racing in this seven-hour event on the bumpy two-mile circuit: "You just had to go as fast as

1960-on tall duplex frame gave CSR fine handling and steering.

Short-lived 1958 600cc G11CSR "Sports Twin".

In 1960 Ron Langston/Don Chapman won overall at Thruxton 500 on an AJS Model 31CSR. The rev counter was an optional extra.

Charismatic but harsh 1958 Matchless G11CSR "Sports Twin", the link to the 650CSRs.

you could without breaking the bike." Which they did, sticking within the recommended rev limit, watching hard-charging Bob McIntyre on the big Enfield fall, making regular stops with ex-racer Monty checking the 650 over, and winning three laps ahead of the nearest Triumph, though as Langston, who rode the last stretch, revealed, by then it was no walkover, as "the clutch was slipping like mad, so we had to ease it along very carefully." Nevertheless they broke the previous year's lap record by 1.6mph, and Langston's final verdict on the CSR was "a nice bike…it went

very well and the handling was OK – certainly better than a Triumph." It was not just a flash in the pan, as for 1963 a G12CSR would win the BRMCC Silverstone 1,000 km race.

These were the peak years for the AMC 650CSRs, 1962 and '63, with the crank-breaking threat over for the newly lively engine. 1962, in addition to the unnecessary naming, had brought the big "knee-knocker" zinc-alloy tank badges. One tester found their trailing edges chafed his knees, and they were undeniably vulgar; but though they had been introduced with a view to cutting expensive chrome-plating on the tanks, as Triumph had done, for 1963 a chrome option was back for the CSR tank, together with a spectacular zig-zag gold-line lightning pattern separating the top panel, painted in Matchless red or AJS blue, from the optional chromed lower part. With this, the badges worked well in a symphony of flash.

The cut-down seat, the beloved alloy guards, preferably unpolished, the open-sided rear light housing, the siamesed exhaust, all made for a temptingly sporty appearance. For the cafés, there were no twinned instruments as standard, but from 1960 a rev counter was an optional extra and could be mounted with the speedo on a separate chromed plate. The '62-on optional downturned bars were a nod in the direction of clip-ons. From May '62 to the end of '63 there was even the factory option of a small fibreglass moulding, a sports cowl surrounding the headlamp, with a fascia and a small flyscreen. There were no twin carbs as standard, but again they could be had from 1962 as part of a race kit, together with 10.25:1 pistons and an even hotter camshaft.

There had been technical as well as cosmetic changes. The rapid wear of camshafts and followers, especially if a twin was used for regular short trips only, was addressed by modifications to the oiling system for 1961, and by the adoption of stellite-tipped cam followers for 1962; their design was improved for 1963, when the width of the oil pumps' gears were doubled to further increase circulation. The gearbox had its long-standing gap between third and top closed up for 1960 (though according to Thruxton CSR racer Bob Doughty, this left a gap between second and third, so that to keep on the power band revs had to go to the maximum before changing up). For 1962 the clutch also was strengthened and gained a fifth plate. 1962 for the CSRs had also seen an alternator replacing the dynamo for secondary electrical functions. 1963 finally brought wider brake shoe linings for the 7-inch drums, which would be widened again for 1964.

Meanwhile however the company's landscape had

shifted, with the old guard of management displaced during 1962 and in 1963 Bill Smith becoming MD of a reconstituted Matchless Motor Cycles. Significantly Smith was a former Sales Director from Norton, and that AMC-owned company had moved in at Plumstead early in the year. On the shop-floor Nortons were known as "the enemy", but that wouldn't stop rationalisation proceeding apace as the domestic market, and sales, shrank dramatically.

Plumstead men were rightly proud of their product with its high standard of engineering and finish (though the superb Forties and Fifties level of paintwork, with "Bonderizing" preparation followed by three coats of best stove-enamelled paint, seemed to have been lost to cost-cutting sometime after 1961, with a 1965 Riders Report on the twins recording paint that faded and wore quickly). Norton was the better known and respected name, but old hands weren't unduly impressed with the Bracebridge Street twin. For example, one quality inspector considered the amount of metal around the Norton engine's valve guides to be insufficient, so that in production everything had to be absolutely precise for the valve guide to line up with the seat; he felt the AMC twins were superior in that respect.

Nevertheless, 1963 was to be the final year for thoroughbred AJS/Matchless twins. Already a Norton-style "cigar" silencer had been introduced during that year. Then for 1964 came the fitting of Roadholder front forks, Norton front wheels with their 8-inch brake, and Norton oil pumps, as well as hybrids powered by the Norton 750 Atlas engine. All these changes made sense in terms of rationalising production and all represented improvements, but the machines' new appearance pleased neither Norton nor AMC fans; they diluted the brands, and in the factory as design engineer Tony Denniss put it, "Matchless had been a well-built machine, so this Norton input was resented."

Model 31CSR 650 c.c.

Hurricane

Renowned high performance coupled with ride-to-work docility make the Hurricane a delightful dual personality machine. Designed primarily for the man who rides fast and far it is the most popular of all fast 650's.

The Plumstead 650 twins had come late to the Rocker ball, trailing tales of cracked cranks and worse than average vibration. Yet the CSRs could be exhilarating machines, free-revving and with strong acceleration to 90 accompanied by their famous "ripping calico" exhaust note on a rising throttle, to make you forget the harsh power delivery and firm suspension. They could be wonderful, dependable motorcycles – if you got a good one. Even more than with other marques, as Harry Winch said, the secret seemed to lie in putting them together properly. The sparkling CSR looked the business, from its beautiful swelling polished alloy cases, to its shining petrol tank and rounded, pannier-style oil tank and toolbox, one of the lightest 650s and looking it. They may never have been mainstream contenders, but for two or three brief years they were a righteous part of the café carnival.

1962 was the Year of The Naming. At least "Hurricane" was a good one.

1968, and the final Matchless CSR, now a G15 with Norton 750 engine, Norton forks, wheels, brakes and silencers, but still in CSR trim. A mean machine whose day was done.

TECHNICAL SPECIFICATIONS:
1963 AJS MODEL 31CSR HURRICANE

Capacity	646cc
Bore	72mm
Stroke	79.3mm
Compression	8.5:1
Power output (claimed)	47.5bhp @ 6200rpm
Electrical system	6 volt
Ignition	Magneto
Generator	Alternator
Wheels and Tyres	F: 3.25 x 19. R: 3.50 x 19
Brakes	F: 7-inch. R: 7-inch
Weight (dry)	381lbs
Top Speed	104mph

RIDE WITH THE ROCKERS

REUNION CAMPING WEEKEND
8, 9, 10, SEPTEMBER 2000

BRIGHTON

RALLY SUNDAY, MADEIRA DRIVE
STRICTLY NO *DECKCHAIRS!*

All enquiries, s.a.e. to: Ace Cafe London, PO Box 3622, London NW4 4AS, England. Tel/Fax: 020 8202 8030. Website: www.ace-cafe london.com